Seeking a New Theology

"Theologians have a long history of promoting schisms. Today the most conspicuous schism is between learning, notably the sciences, and belief. David Marshall's *Seeking a New Theology* aims to mend this schism and the enormous confusion and wrongs that result from it. His is not a prescription for a new belief cure-all. It is an open invitation to explore the variety of religious beliefs in light of new scientific mysteries able to evoke an innovative, more comprehensive, and more credible basis for belief."

—EMILIO DEGRAZIA
Author of *Seventeen Grams of Soul*

"Theology and science are often viewed as antagonists, totally different ways of understanding reality. David Marshall, however, sees them as potential partners. His remarkably understandable descriptions of insights from astrophysics to quantum mechanics offer hints that might enlighten long-held theological beliefs. Marshall's finely honed skills as a teacher clarify diverse subjects, from Eastern religions to scientific views about whether life (consciousness) survives death. He offers highly informed perspectives by which to reexamine one's own understanding."

—RICHARD DAHL
Winona State University

"This book is for all who question how faith and science can engage, enhance, and evolve the other. Through theological questions, biblical texts, perspectives from major world religions, and accessible scientific explanations, Marshall's ability to 'open doors' between faith and science captures the creative tension of how faith and science can simultaneously expose limitations and expand possibilities for 'probing the mysteries of God's creation.'"

—DEANNA LANGLE
Retired Campus Pastor, Lutheran Campus
Ministry at Northwestern University

"If certain topics need to be addressed at this time, *Seeking a New Theology* is one. The pressing religious questions of our age are pertinent to understanding our social, political, and environmental problems. David Marshall steps in with relevant, cogent indicators toward answers! He has examined the widespread, insufficient contemporary understanding in a special way—with compassion, pointing to our 'propositional uncertainty.' That the author has thought long and hard about these issues is self-evident. Additionally, there is a genius of expression on his part, engaging us in his terse, often witty, writing. . . ."

—**DAVID ROOMY**
Union Theological Seminary

"David Marshall's delightful, broad-ranging, accessible, question-stimulating book can benefit (1) the increasing number of younger people raised with no religious background but who are curious about it; (2) those skeptical of established religious traditions but who consider themselves to be 'spiritual'; (3) individuals hurt by the narrowness of their religious upbringing; and (4) believers still within a tradition seeking to expand more inclusively and generously what it means to 'believe.'"

—**TIMOTHY FORESTER**
Retired Congregational pastor, United Church of Christ

Seeking a New Theology

Some Hints on What Science Might
Enlighten in Theology

David F. Marshall

RESOURCE *Publications* • Eugene, Oregon

SEEKING A NEW THEOLOGY
Some Hints on What Science Might Enlighten in Theology

Copyright © 2021 David F. Marshall. All rights reserved. Except for brief quotations in critical publications or reviews, no part of this book may be reproduced in any manner without prior written permission from the publisher. Write: Permissions, Wipf and Stock Publishers, 199 W. 8th Ave., Suite 3, Eugene, OR 97401.

Resource Publications
An Imprint of Wipf and Stock Publishers
199 W. 8th Ave., Suite 3
Eugene, OR 97401

www.wipfandstock.com

PAPERBACK ISBN: 978-1-6667-0319-1
HARDCOVER ISBN: 978-1-6667-0320-7
EBOOK ISBN: 978-1-6667-0321-4

08/03/21

All Scriptural Quotations from The New Oxford Annotated Bible with the Apocrypha, Revised Standard Version, Herbert G. May and Bruce M. Metzger, editors. New York: Oxford University Press, 1977.

My wife Ruth's contributions were blessings, keeping me balanced to the finish, and it is dedicated to her with love, and also to our two sons, Michael, a help always with his good advice, much which I probably should have followed, and Nathan, helping more than he knows, undaunted by "the slings and arrows of outrageous fortune" while aiding people in these hard times.

Contents

Images | ix
Acknowledgements | xi
Introduction: What This Book Is About | xiii

Section One: Science and Theology as Dance Partners | 1
   Chapter 1: Naming the Deity | 3
   Chapter 2: Studying the Divine—Theology | 5
   Chapter 3: The Focus (or Locus) of Theology | 7
   Chapter 4: Problems of Writing About God | 10
   Chapter 5: Scripture's Historical Accuracy? | 13
   Chapter 6: Using the Saints as a Source | 15
   Chapter 7: Some Problems with Christmas | 18
   Chapter 8: Early Church Fathers | 20
   Chapter 9: The Dilemma of Theodicy | 23
   Chapter 10: Science vs. Theology | 27
   Chapter 11: Science as a Good Source | 30
   Chapter 12: Where We Are in the Universe | 33
   Chapter 13: Looking Down Inside Creation | 36
   Chapter 14: Using Einstein's Discoveries | 38
   Chapter 15: It's About Time, and So is God | 45
   Chapter 16: One of Science's Uncivil Battles | 48
   Chapter 17: Some Solutions about Quanta | 51
   Chapter 18: Regarding Absolutes | 53
   Chapter 19: Regarding Constants | 56

Section Two: Questions About Avatars—Gods Who Become Human | 59
   Chapter 20: Human Deities or Avatars | 61
   Chapter 21: War Leader Avatars in Islam? | 65

Chapter 22: Hinduism: Many Avatars | 68
Chapter 23: Jainism: All Life is Holy | 71
Chapter 24: Shinto: Ritual, Kami, Nature | 74
Chapter 25: Confucianism: Being Respectful | 76
Chapter 26: Taoism: Sensitivity to All | 78
Chapter 27: Sikhism: Serving, Living, Duty | 82
Chapter 28: Bahá'í: Synoptic Goals—Seeking Peace | 85
Chapter 29: Judaism: Being Chosen Has a Price | 87
Chapter 30: Christianity I: Avatar's Time/Place | 90
Chapter 31: Christianity II: Avatar's Gender | 94
Chapter 32: Christianity III: Avatar's People | 97
Chapter 33: Christianity IV: Many Messiahs and Many Views | 99
Chapter 34: Christianity V: Humanity vs. Deity | 104
Chapter 35: Christianity VI: Pro Avatar Reasons | 108

Section Three: Some Recent Scientific Discoveries of Interest and Importance | 111
Chapter 36: What's Below Atoms | 113
Chapter 37: A Word of Caution About Doors | 117
Chapter 38: FRBs: An Example of a Trap | 119
Chapter 39: Us, the Stars and Their Energy | 122
Chapter 40: Possible Answers to Questions | 126
Chaper 41: Gravitational Waves to the Rescue | 130
Chapter 42: Visible Proof of Black Holes | 134
Chapter 43: Some More Advances in Science | 136
Chapter 44: Neutrinos and the Urca Process | 139
Chapter 45: Survival of Information | 142
Chapter 46: Perhaps the Greatest Question | 146
Chapter 47: Life After Death—Con | 148
Chapter 48: Life After Death—Pro | 150
Chapter 49: Life After Death—Some Details | 153
Chapter 50: Life From Another Perspective | 157
Chapter 51: A View from Analytical Psychology | 160

An Afterword | 163
Endnotes | 165
Bibliography | 171

Images

Cover: Cover cartoon is copyright © by Crowden Satz, used by permission.

1. NASA: "Gravity Probe B and Space-Time." https://www.nasa.gov/mission_pages/gpb_012.hyml. 16257main_GPB_circling_earth3_516.jpg. | 39
2. "Last Jew in Vinnitza," https://en.wikipidia.org/index.php?title=The_Last_Jew_in_Vinnitza&oldid=994979106.the_last_jew_in_vinnitza,_1941.jpg. | 42
3. Library of Congress/United States Holocaust Museum/Bundesarchiv–Bild–Ac0706–018030–Ukraine–emordete–Familie.jpg. | 43
4. Two neutron stars colliding; Eso1733s University of Warwick/Mark Garlick, Wikipedia. | 54
5. "Steps at Tai Shan," updated. Nov.6, 2020.https://en.wikipedia.org/w/index. php?title=Mount_Tai&oldid=98703862. | 80
6. Mass–energy-pie-chart. Berkeley Lab. Glen Roberts Jr. "3 Known and 3 Unknowns about Dark Mater," May 24, 2016. | 116 & 127
7. "Chronology of the Universe" https://en.wikipedia.org/w/index. php?title= Chronology_of_the_Universe&oldid=1004470520. updated Feb. 2, 2021. "Timeline of the Universe." CMB_Timeline300_no_WMAP.jpg. | 128
8. "First Image of a Black Hole." Image: Event Horizon Telescope Collaboration. "How Scientists Captured the First Image of a Black Hole," Ota Lutz.jpl.nasa.gov. | 135
9. A rupture in the crust of a highly magnetized neutron star, shown here in an artist's rendering, can trigger high-energy eruptions.

Images

Observations of these blasts include information on how the star's surface twists and vibrates, providing new insights into what lies beneath. Credits: NASA's Goddard Space Flight Center/S. Wiessinger. | 141

Acknowledgements

Dr. Emilio De Grazia of Winona State University was helpful in proofing reading; his advice as an often published poet greatly improved the text, the framing of topics and the flow of ideas and arguments.

David Roomy, Jungian counselor, first to read a draft, his encouragement often reinforced my determination all the way from Vancouver, BC.

Dr. Deanna Langle, a campus minister, advised against some too-light-hearted comments, and also counseled me on how to write for students.

Richard K. Dahl, who truly lives his faith, contributed with new interpretations of the Incarnation, helping put the transhistorical into clearer perspective.

Theodore Haaland, also a poet, aided me as one writer to another.

The Rev. Timothy Forester, with many chats over coffee, undergirded my theological fascination, putting ideas forward which were motivating.

Introduction

What This Book Is About

Worthy reader, this tome is written for those who sometimes sit in pews, even if only for a day or two each year, who say "I believe" but their minds really respond, "Maybe I don't think so." Also, it is for those who find science really fascinating but sometimes feel they're not quite completely understanding very well. It could interest those not familiar with questions of theology but wanting to learn more, as well as those non-scientists hoping to understand more about quantum mechanics and astrophysics. It is also written for those who want to enjoy wrapping their minds around theological complexities and are curious about how science might unknot some of those tangled concepts and doctrines. Last but definitely not least, it is written for all who look out at the universe's night sky and wonder how it was made, when, and by Whom.

SECTION ONE

Science and Theology as Dance Partners

WE BEGIN BY ASKING where our theology comes from. When closely examined, theology's sources have reliability issues such as the validity of some biblical scriptures and their accuracy, the problems of the witness of saints, mistakes in the timing of biblical events and celebrations, even whether evidence from church fathers and councils can be relied upon. We then examine science to see if it can help solve some major questions in theology; a good example is *theodicy*, that is: How can God be all good and, at the same time, all powerful? Using an easily understood discovery by Einstein, we arrive at a possible solution. With that reassurance, we seek to discover if the universe has constants, things that are always to be relied upon, or any absolutes, things that are sure to happen always.

With those issues contended with, we can then move on to another section where we take a look at some questions in other religions besides Christianity.

Chapter 1

Naming the Deity

Before we begin, we need to get one major problem out of the way. How do people refer to the Divine Being? People speak of the deity in many ways: Often as "Father," less often as "(Great) Mother" or the "Lord." These terms take us back to medieval times or even earlier, signifying or suggesting a myriad of other names.

When humans first started believing in something greater than themselves, they chose a source of power such as thunder, lightning and storms, and later they linked deity to pharaohs, kings, nobles, potentates or emperors. Medieval Names for God abounded, such as Lord and . . . ? The list goes on and on, but Lord is masculine; it is not Lady, and it designates gender.

How dare we really ascribe these gendered titles to our God, for that would be somewhat conceited at best? How do we know? What if we got it wrong? Is it really necessary for God to have a gender? After careful thought, we might need to say, "Probably not!"

To solve this problem, let's agree to designate the deity as God to avoid absurd psychological projection of gender. Please notice that this name is capitalized for obvious reasons. Remember, some people even regard the utterance of God's biblical name as sacrilegious, perhaps even a major sin. As in so many situations, it depends upon context.

If the deity's appellation is "God," then you can't take the real name in vain. (see Exodus 3:14). Perhaps the deity name might be a verb, just as R. Buckminster Fuller felt himself to be in the title of his book, *I Seem to Be a Verb*.[1]

Section One: Science and Theology as Dance Partners

Making the deity's name a verb is rather difficult. One suggestion that makes sense is to refer to God's major undertaking—*Creating*—so a good name might be Creator. The Hebrew name of God is also good in one of its translations—*Isness* or *Being*. The theologian Paul Tillich referred to God as "the ground of being."

CHAPTER 2

Studying the Divine—Theology

SINCE WE'RE DISCUSSING GOD, we need to understand what our study of divinity entails—theology. The word means, when broken down linguistically, "the study of the divine." The two morphemes (a group of sounds that make up meaningful parts of a word) are *theos*- referring to the Greek word for "gods" and *–ology* from Greek *logos* referring to "word, study or speech." Thus, its linguistic roots mean speaking or studying about god(s). Since before the time of the Delphic Oracle, where Greeks and others went to find out what their gods had to say about their affairs or problems, persons have been said to hear deities speak to them; unfortunately, there are no sound tracks to verify such, although there are some people who claim to have heard god(s) often. The Greeks were polytheists (believers in more than one god), and they claimed that Apollo spoke through the Delphic Oracle. It was she, Apollo's priestess, who said the Greeks would defeat the Persians behind "a wooden wall," which turned out to be their fleet of ships at the Battle of Salamis (480 BCE).

There seems to be an historical parade of persons speaking for or as God(s) demanding to be heard. That's a major problem because we need some verification or proof of authenticity. Therein abides the major problem for all prophets, real or not. They do not have an audience without their listener's willingness to listen.

To claim to converse with the deity seems somewhat conceited and highly questionable at best, and dependent on a person's mental balance, at worst. However, some people will claim almost anything for a

Section One: Science and Theology as Dance Partners

staggering multiplicity of reasons, but that does not mean that what's said is true or provable.

A person's opinions may be his or her own, but facts are available to all of us and are always collective. Water is wet; that's a fact, not a belief or opinion. In several religions it was and in some is still believed that anyone who sees God(s) seems to immediately die; however, hearing the divine for some persons appears to be different, more easily realized, on occasion, and definitely not fatal.

That very act of listening or conversing is most interesting. Hearing is often utilized if communicating with the deity; however, use of the other senses doesn't come very readily into the proposition, for who could say: "I touched God" (perhaps for Christians it might be St. Thomas verifying Jesus's stigmata) or (*may God please forgive the idea*) "I smelled the divine." The improbability of these claims demonstrates the absurdity of using human senses in claiming divine communication. I'm not even going to mention the sense of taste, for such would be totally absurd; however, a good pecan pie can seem almost heavenly and is definitely a blessing, and please notice—when consumed, it involves our senses, but only in seldom occasions does it through rumbles answer back.

God made a plethora of huge dark holes centering millions of galaxies and created myriads of exploding novas that might be as dangerous to meet as these celestial phenomena, and they have been scientifically posited, seen, some even heard, but none tasted, touched or smelled. Relying on our senses when approaching the deity for understanding often seems futile on one hand and dangerous on the other. Perhaps the best meeting is a meeting of the minds; this event has a name—it is called prayer.

Neil de Grasse Tyson noted, "When scientifically investigating the natural world, the only thing worse than a blind believer is a seeing denier."[2] Surely that insight holds true for theology as well. Blind believers might seem to be good, but they seem to deny God's gift of a reasoning brain, and seeing deniers reject their God-given powers of thought and sense and the blessings of awe.

You can now appreciate one of the many problems of theology; it is a very complex subject to study. Is it too complex? Nor really! God seems to want to be better known.

Chapter 3

The Focus (or Locus) of Theology

You might wonder what *theology* means? How do we get it, and when, then how do we understand what it is that we have? The answer largely depends upon your specific religion or selected branch or branch of a branch (and sometimes there are many) of whatever religion you are studying. That makes each theology the product of a specific brand (flavor?) of religion. How do you choose a religion or theology? The decisions you make, in no small way, mold and fashion how you perceive the deity (or deities) and what you do when you make theories about your pondered objectives.

No God or one God or many gods? This question divides the religions of the world into major categories. We see a spectrum, from no god to a multitude, depending upon which to choose. If the many, then: Who tells whom what to do? Who is in charge? Is there a hierarchy of god(s) or priests? A person studying a particular belief system would find that a plethora of differing theologies might begin to appear, each with the potentiality of marked hostility toward the others. Not surprisingly, that outcome in the study of religion rather often has been the case. Even with only one God—as in Islam, for example—there is still hostility and bloodshed between factions; the same was true also in Christianity. Consider the Christian Crusaders sacking Constantinople, a Christian capital (1204) or the Thirty-Years War between Catholics and Protestants (1618–1648) that fostered multiple war crimes (estimated deaths: 4.5 to 8 Million). Generation after generation has seen religious warfare.

Section One: Science and Theology as Dance Partners

Thinking of this infighting in religions, we might ask: What if there is no God or god(s)? Without a *theo* or its plural, you would technically have no *theology*, only a *logy*. What you would have is a collection of rules for behavior, that is, an *ethics*.

When we have only an ethics, we would find ourselves perhaps interested in philosophy, not theology. Please note that there are some with university degrees in ethics who say ethics is not a subdivision of theology. Ethics does not require a deity, only an idea of the "Good" or "doing good." Perhaps even those two ideas are different. The "Good" is something "out there or in here somewhere" that one takes directions from; such a mental construct is singular and capable of enhancing all of life. "Doing good" is personal or corporate, national or international action regarding other entities. Today, we are beginning to realize that such "doing good" may extend to the inanimate as well as the animate, even to the environment itself, but for now, we need to see that a *theology* does require and presupposes a deity, although you can have a belief system that leaves the question of deity totally unidentified.

A deity–less theology could create multiple problems, were it not carefully articulated. There is such a belief system, a major one, as we will see later. For those who don't want or feel they do need deity, do stick with our discussion a little longer; it might enhance your ideas. No, you won't be subjected to attempts at conversion! That's not ethical! Each person has the inherent right to decide his or her own theology without outside pressure or coercion. In Judaism, a person proselytizing manifests a sin.

What seems to be overlooked often in theology is the basic human right for the individual to choose as well as the right to change one's mind after that choice results from further study. Why do some people not let others make up their own minds? That inherent right to make our own decisions is a major and foundational element of anyone's theological search. Would you burn or execute someone who disagrees with you about how your deity is worshiped? That error has happened too often. Persons have been hanged, starved to death, stoned, tortured to death or slaughtered in many other ways because they did not worship as some group thought they should. Such is still happening, even today, in the Middle East, Africa, and elsewhere, including the United States where worshippers recently were gunned down in a synagogue.

One wonders what causes some theologians to forget fundamental human rights when trying to convince others of the validity of their views.

The Focus (or Locus) of Theology

We're going to see some more of that conceit the deeper we go into our exploration of seeking a new theology, a conceit not limited to any one religion, but one, unfortunately, rather wide-spread.

Do some religious people sometimes sell eternal insurance for the soul that might not seem to cost money (although too often it probably does in contributions), just their devotion and actions while they are living? True faith is more than post-life insurance for eternity.

There are many propositions regarding truth; perhaps some of us are too easily swayed. Theologians sometimes have not seriously researched the values of the propositional uncertainty in faith, and religious leaders should thoroughly study such concepts to honestly help those who come inquiring. With faith also arrives doubt, for it lacks surety, a necessity that keeps it from being knowledge.

Should we dare to censor anyone who does not agree with us about what all can only hope for? Just because you believe in something doesn't necessarily mean you are right and those who believe differently are wrong. "To believe" is a very well-defined verb; one of its antonyms—its opposite—is "to prove." There is a sharp difference between proving something and believing something. If we believe something and do not know it for fact, that's the essence of faith. Notice Hebrews 11:1—12:2, a scriptural essay which seems somewhat sound, for it defines faith, not through beliefs but through a persons's actions. Action does have far more power than words.

One should disapprove of proof texts—biblical texts used in arguments to prove a point; often, they are used out of context. Having faith not only concerns what you have; it also concerns what you seek to have and often what your actions demonstrate. People can be convinced of almost anything, but their conviction, no matter how deeply felt, does not guarantee the truth of a belief. Faith is something that lives without its own self-validation. It is rejoicing in the unproved, and that makes it also markedly nonscientific. You might be surprised later to see what scientists believe to be true, but sometimes are lacking proof. The difference between science and religious belief is not as far apart as some believe.

CHAPTER 4

Problems of Writing About God

THEOLOGY CLAIMS TO BE founded on scriptures and commentaries on those writings. A careful reading of history shows that there were some serious quarrels over just what was scripture and what was not. Even if we accept the writings we now have, some scholars claim that scripture is directly received from God. For an example from one religion, not all early believers in the first centuries of Christianity agreed about what should be included as scripture. You only have to research the Council of Laodicea (363), the Council of Hippo (393) or the Council of Carthage (397) to see the arguments about what books went into the Bible. Editions of the Bible don't, even today, agree on the book titles; just compare the titles of the books in a Catholic and a Protestant Bible.

Given these differences regarding what is scripture, why don't we honestly examine the claim made by some that the deity wrote, that is, actually authored, each and every one of the scriptures? There can be no dispute that god(s) inspired scriptures in many if not most religions, but inspiration is not the same as actual authorship. If mistakes arise, we must ask who made them and how. Errors, even in scripture, are not uncommon. Here are a few examples for us to examine.

Almost all religions claim that their deity does not make mistakes; however, were the deity of the New Testament the author of those texts, some texts seem to err. This is true down to the level of grammar. One might squirm when watching a professional football game and seeing a placard in the stands reading: *"The wages of sin is death"* (a quote from Romans 6:23 in the New Testament). Not even Ms Nose, my first-grade elementary teacher,

Problems of Writing About God

would dare correct that sentence, given its provenance, but you know in your heart that it is ungrammatical (flagrant subject–verb disagreement; plural subject, singular verb). Does this mean that God made a grammar error? Some would argue that the error results from mistakes by copyists, but even the very earliest manuscripts of Romans 6:23 show the error. Maybe Paul in writing Romans made the error, but if Paul did err, then God didn't do the writing, only inspiring Paul's authorship but not dictating the wording. Inspiration differs from writing, and authors make mistakes.

A person could argue that the problem arrives through a translation error. Unfortunately, that is not so. The error is in the Greek manuscripts of Romans as well. At this time we need to relax and simply say to ourselves regarding whether God wrote the scriptures or not, "Houston, we have a problem," especially regarding authorship of scripture by a deity. Why can't we recognize that writing scripture is a human activity, and that it can often suffer from the pain and perils of our too human weaknesses? Scripture as information is transmitted, and there appear to be transmission errors, some subtle, some gross.

Another example is from the *Tenach* (Jewish name for the Old Testament) in 1 Kings 7:23; it reads that King Solomon's Temple is stated to have had a large bowl or tank. It was round with measurements of 10 cubits from brim to brim and a circumference of 30 cubits. That means the concept of pi (π), which is an infinite succession of non-repeating digits (3.141592653979323...) used to find the circumference of a circle, is in this verse only the number 3 (30 divided by 10). If you were wondering, a cubit is an ancient measure from middle finger to elbow, usually 17 to 22 inches, depending on who is doing the measuring. After all, God is said to have created mathematics including pi (π), which is more accurate than a cubit.

Constituting a theology on one's scriptural interpretation alone can be problematic many times, resulting in errors at best and "nit-picking" at worse.

Seeking a new theology while attempting an exegesis reading of sacred writings is not exactly a foolproof endeavor. Too often it is not *exegesis* (reading *from*) but *eisegesis* or *isogesis* (reading *into* to match your ideas). Perhaps we need to remember the lyrics of George and Ira Gershwin's aria from their opera, *Porgy and Bess*: "It Ain't Necessarily So." Its lyrics suggest there are several biblical stories that might not be accurately described. Ira Gershwin isn't denying the Bible; he's just raising a humorous sense of doubt about how scriptures were written, given our human condition and tendency to make errors.

Speaking of doubt, in Tennessee, Noah's Ark recently has been reconstructed using the directions found in Genesis 6:15–16. I wonder where these modern builders got "gopher wood"? Does anyone know what it is? During the 2019 floods, the Ark Corporation filed insurance claims because a flood damaged the newly built Ark.

Yes, skepticism of unfounded claims can be healthy for your uncertainty, and if such claims are thought through wisely regarding possible errancy in scripture, skepticism might be helpful to your faith, for it reinforces your exegesis and not your eisegesis. We need to read the scriptures very carefully and with as much objectivity and guidance from a number of scholars as numerous as humanly possible.

There still stands a larger problem concerning divine will. As the African-American traditional spiritual "Didn't My Lord Deliver Daniel" lyrics state:

> He delivered Daniel from the lion's den,
> Jonah from the belly of the whale,
> And the Hebrew children from the fiery furnace, and why not every man?
> *Chorus:*
> Didn't my Lord deliver Daniel, deliver Daniel, deliver Daniel,
> Didn't my Lord deliver Daniel, and why not every man?

The question arises: Why are so few saved from death and not the millions of others? It's a question that confronts us squarely, but we need to search long and hard to find a satisfactory one in today's theology. Why is that question not more pondered? This question of whether God seems to play "favorites" and ignores others is one of the top questions asked by those who have lost their faith or are in great doubt and now have abandoned organized religion. Saying the answer is a mystery only dodges the question. There are many people who want an answer and there exists a need for theologians to find one.

CHAPTER 5

Scripture's Historical Accuracy?

THE MANUSCRIPTS OF SCRIPTURES do have errors in grammar and word meanings, but they also err in word reference. A good example can be found in the *Book of Proverbs* in the King James Version of the Bible [1611], perhaps the most popular biblical version in Protestant churches in the past four centuries. The King James Version states that even the king's palace had *spiders*. Careful recent scholarship has discovered that the Hebrew word which was translated in 1611 as "spiders" in Proverbs 30:28 actually refers to *lizards*, and modern translations have been changed accordingly. Is this God's inerrancy in writing the Bible? Not likely! The word existed in Hebrew, the language in which the Old Testament was written. Is it a 1611 translators's error? Absolutely!

Scriptures also have errors regarding historic events and astronomical references. The latter is mentioned here because some believe that the event described during the crucifixion was an eclipse. The name Jesus is a Greek transliteration; he was known in Hebrew as Yeshua ben Yosef, the carpenter's son from Nazareth. In Luke 23:44, it is written that he died, and then, "There was a darkness over all the Earth." Was this evidence of an eclipse? Careful modern translation from the Greek informs us that the phrase is "darkness over all the land," not "all the Earth." Hyperbole does appear in scripture often enough to make us skeptical of some claims. An eclipse would seem to make sense until we check further, scientifically. It is rather easy to find out if an eclipse was possible within that time frame. The one that did occur presents major problems for gospel chronology. Luke 3:1–4 says that the ministry of John the Baptist began in the fifteenth year of the reign of Emperor Tiberius, which was the year 29 of the Current Era (CE). Yes, there was an eclipse on November 24, 29 CE, but that means that there was less than a year for John the Baptist and Jesus to have had their ministries. The majority of scholars don't argue about how long Jesus's ministry lasted; almost all say about three years. The supposed eclipse is also mentioned in the gospels of Matthew and Mark.[3]

Were all three synoptic gospel writers, Matthew, Mark, and Luke, remembering an event and putting it into the present in their gospels? The time frame for an eclipse just doesn't fit otherwise, and if that is so, then where do we go for more accurate information in scripture when seeking a plausible theology? That scripture can be erroneous shouldn't create disbelief in all records of religions around the world. Where we should go is to experts in scriptural languages and histories, to scholars who have studied and proposed alternative readings. Good scholarship admits errors when they are found. Humans err, far too often, when dealing with the divine.

With some scriptural references and allusions sometimes questionable, we perhaps, when we seek a more accurate theology, can turn to something else more consistent than scriptures that were written and possibly recorded from memory, copied and recopied from memory time after time, probably with human errors and written mistakenly when we seek a more accurate theology. In the case of the eclipses, the correct information about eclipses came from science, from astronomy, not from ancient and translated scriptures.

Science could help us reinterpret scriptures more accurately. Shouldn't we utilize it to make our theology clearer and more believable?

Chapter 6

Using the Saints as a Source

ANOTHER SOURCE FOR OUR theologies comes from what is called "the witness of the saints"; unfortunately, we find numerous problems with this type of study, which is called *hagiography*, the writings about the holy ones; that is—*hagio-*(holy); *-graphy* (writing).

When I was a lad in West Texas, on many automobile dashboards there was a statue of St. Christopher, a Roman soldier, patron saint of travelers. Today there are not so many, for in 1969 Christopher was "dropped" from the *Calendarium Romanum*, the official Roman Catholic calendar of feast days for saints and other religious events.[4]

St. Christopher's sainthood was questioned, along with that of others such as the crucial-to-Christmas St. Nicholas, our inspiration for Santa Claus. The hagiography of St. Nicholas is under further intensive study. In all, over 131 saints were "dropped" from the calendar in 1969.[5] This type of saint "misremembrance" is nothing new. There were a number of Celtic saints dropped after the Irish and other Celtic churches came under the direct governance of the Bishop of Rome. At the Synod of Whitby, 663–64, the Celtic clergy were ecclesiastically voted under Rome's aegis, losing, over time, their Celtic rites, tonsures, coed monasteries and other unique differences from Rome, most notably the dating of Easter.[6]

Please do remember, a saint cannot be erased from the roll of saints—once a saint, always a saint, but saints can have their feast days dropped from the official *Calendarium Romanum* and their suspected hagiographies severely questioned. Their veneration cannot cease over the years, but it may be severely curtailed. There are many supposed saints without fully verified documentation whose hagiographies remain under further highly critical study. Some of these Vatican studies might, over time, prove to be very instructive.

One of the more suspect hagiographies is that of St. Ursula and the 11,000 Virgins. It was taught that near Cologne the Huns massacred her and supposedly her accompanying 11,000 virgins. The mind boggles as to how Ursula, supposedly a British king's daughter, recruited 11,000 virgins in one of the small early medieval rural kingdoms in England. Other sources claim 60,000 other women were also massacred. These sources for the supposed slaughter date from more than 400 years after the proposed time of the incident. This hagiography seems to depend mostly on an old inscription in the Cathedral at Cologne, one extremely difficult to read or to accurately decode.[7]

Another exceptional saint, to say the least, is St. Simeon Stylites (c. 390–459), one of the Egyptian desert saints who become a pillar hermit, a recluse who sat on a pillar for many decades. A monk, he was expelled from his monastery, but because it had been rumored that he could perform miracles, crowds pestered him until he retreated to the top of a *style*, a pillar, and lived there day and night for the rest of his life. His first pillar was only six feet high, but over the years he moved higher and higher, slowly graduating to a fifty-foot pillar. He inspired many others, women and men, to imitate his austerities while sitting in the desert to be seen by everyone below. Stylites, people who sit on pillars for various religious reasons, were associated with churches and lasted until the nineteenth century in Russia. In the deserts of the Middle East, it might seem possible to survive on the top of a pillar, but being a stylite in a Russian winter seems certifiably insane and deadly.[8]

The stylites had food delivered via baskets so they would not have to descend; personal hygiene also probably remained a major problem. With their sense of superb showmanship, a real chance for gaining theological insight illuminated by these saintly sitters seems to gain more and more skepticism as it is studied. Obviously, the practice was discontinued.

One might wonder what psychiatrists would have to say about these pillar sitters. To those saints we should add also the sometimes exaggerated, questionable saints's hagiographies, that is, those allegations about saints whose activities raise historical doubt even for some authorities in the Catholic Church.

Using the Saints as a Source

Doesn't belief require at least a modicum of factuality? Does not our taking our belief seriously require that we investigate any and all sources from which that belief derives?

CHAPTER 7

Some Problems with Christmas

WHILE WE ARE DISCUSSING saints' days, what about that major holiday called Christmas, which has customers crashing into stores immediately after Thanksgiving in order to purchase gifts? Yes, what about the origin of Christmas, without which the economy would suffer greatly?

Christmas is argued to be the holiday that celebrates Jesus's birth in Bethlehem. According to Luke 2:8–20, shepherds were guarding their flocks in the fields. If the date for Christmas is correct, then it was stark winter. Surely then, wasn't it too cold to be out, both for shepherds and sheep? Weren't the sheep in the mangers and barns to keep them warm and thus not freeze to death? Were there sheep in Bethlehem's manger?

Also, did not the Magi follow the star in the east to get to the stable and give their gifts, as told in Matthew 2:1–12? These Three Magi, that is, wise men from the East, wouldn't they have traveled West to get to Judea? These magi or sages were later popularly elevated to kings in the following centuries, and some of their relics supposedly ended up in Cologne Cathedral in the twelfth century, the same locale for the St. Ursula story.[9]

We need to remember that Christmas was declared Jesus's birthday about 300 years after the Crucifixion. Christmas was established as a holiday coming a few days after the winter solstice—at that time when you can notice that the days are slightly getting longer. There were many other winter solstice celebrations in other areas and in other religions. and that might be the reason. There is a long list and here are a few examples. The Romans had a week of orgies called Saturnalia, which featured extensive celebration of the Unconquered Sun. Celtic tribes celebrated with festivities around Yule logs. Teutonic tribes supposedly added the Christmas tree, which apparently developed from St. Boniface, a major missionary to the Teutons who replaced the sacred oak of Odin with a decorated fir tree.[10] Other legends clustering around December 25 include those of Good King Wenceslaus, Kwanza and especially Saint Nicholas, who lived in what now is present-day Turkey. The custom of gift giving in this season of the winter solstice dates to far earlier times than the Incarnation in Bethlehem. Were these the reasons why the church selected the winter date instead of one more favorable to shepherds?

If Christmas, a major church festival, is not when Jesus was born, do we dare trust other questionable dates in the calendar of the church? It seems church authorities might have "fudged" on the date of the Jesus's birth, perhaps to counter a dominant Roman pagan holiday. The date for Easter has also been debated, and it took church councils until the seventh century to set the final date by a rather complex method. What is evident is that we cannot take some dates propagated by the church as being historically accurate, unfortunately not even Easter. I learned from a rabbi that the initial celebration of the Last Supper in the upper room, thought by many to have been an early Seder marking Passover, was really a celebration of a Jewish Spring planting festival. He was able to point out that the Seder for Passover was instituted around a century and a half after the Crucifixion.

Perhaps we need to adopt a more scientific attitude toward the dates and pronouncements that are so treasured in current theology, particularly those reinforced by social custom and just plain habit. Theology is too serious to be based on custom and habit.

CHAPTER 8

Early Church Fathers

IF NOT THE SAINTS (God bless them all!) or holidays, what about the noted Church Fathers, those early theologians who labored to work out the question of just how much of Jesus was deity, that is, holy, and how much just a human person? Let's examine a church father termed "the most important theologian and biblical scholar of the early Greek church."[11]

It was alleged, probably falsely by Eusebius, fourth century author of *Ecclesiastical History*, that Origen (ca. 185–ca. 254), as a young man, castrated himself in order to be able chastely to teach females about the faith. This gossip probably resulted from later attacks on him. Such an attack came later from his friend, Heraclas, a colleague while they were students but later his foe and rival, who, after he become Bishop of Alexandria, refused Origen the sacrament.

With the help of a wealthy sponsor, whom he had converted and who paid for the shorthand scribes, Origen produced his major works: *Miscellanies; On the Resurrection; On First Principles,* and a copious commentary *On St. John,* arguing in 32 books against Gnostic interpretations of the gospels, the heresy that taught a demiurge had made the world and had the human spirit trapped inside bodies needing certain knowledge (in Greek, *gnosis*) to get out. In Christianity, however, faith, not knowledge or *gnosis,* has always been deemed to be primary.

One of his major works was the *Hexapla,* an examination of various versions of the Old Testament: Hebraic, Greek, Latin, Aramaic and others. Its breadth is truly staggering, and it remains a major theological document, even today. The work illustrates Origen's perhaps liberal but careful interpretations regarding theological concepts. His only self-requirement was that his philosophical speculations did not become heretical and remained steadfastly within Christianity, no matter the source or the thinker's socioeconomic background. Origen in his *Contra Celsum*, argued:

> [A] philosophic mind has a right to think within a Christian framework and that the Christian faith is neither a prejudice of the unreasoning masses nor a crutch for social outcasts or nonconformists. (Origen quoted in Chadwick)

Even with this broadmindedness, Origen was attacked, not only by skeptics but also by other Christian theologians and some church hierarchs. He was charged with many heresies during his life and afterwards. In 543, Emperor Justinian I issued an edict denouncing Origen, and it was extended that year at the Fifth Ecumenical Council. However, Origen is still read today in seminaries as one of the major and very insightful Church Fathers. Chadwick writes: "There is much reason to justify Jerome's first judgment that Origen was the greatest teacher of the early church after the Apostles." St. Jerome (347–420) was the Church Father responsible for translating the scriptures in the Vulgate, the Latin version of the Bible that became the official version for the Catholic Church for many centuries.

On his travels, Origen was imprisoned and tortured during Emperor Decius's persecution (around 250). Origin died a few years later.

Origin shows us the irony that arises when we see his life's problems. Although he is now regarded as one of the most outstanding interpreters of theology in the early church, he was very badly treated by the church he loved. Do we want to go sifting through the dusty pages of the Church Fathers for our theology? There are some who deserve our reading and extended study. There are also other examples of unjustly persecuted Church Fathers. It seems they were not exactly a happy group, disagreeing often about major problems and involved in sad incidents, even of violence, at early church councils and synods.

Reading detailed narratives of the early church councils reveals marked anger, caustic argument, acrimonious denunciation and sometimes even the inflicting of personal injury.[12] For examples, research these: First Council of Constantinople, 381; First Council of Ephesus, 431; Second Council of Ephesus, 449, the so-called "Robbers Council." Some of these councils were rowdy, often loud, argumentative, vituperative, vitriolic in dialogue and could be infrequently violent. For an example, look up the Second Council of Ephesus, the "Robbers Council."[13]

Section One: Science and Theology as Dance Partners

Perhaps in seeking a new theology, we might do better to seek our insights elsewhere and carefully parse the arguments arising in the first six centuries of the church councils. What the councils promulgated was very often crucial theologically, but the methodology was often rude and sometimes violent. In some instances, it was "miraculous" any work got done at all, which tells us a lot. Leaders of the early church were truly just as human with their failings and problems as other people who have sought theological enlightenment through the centuries.

CHAPTER 9

The Dilemma of Theodicy

THE ARGUMENTS AMONG THE early church fathers were primarily about the nature of the Incarnation, that is, what part of Jesus was human and what part was deity: body, soul or both? The problem is significant, since to be human meant automatically to be liable to sin through Adam, while God was above and incapable of sin. The question underlies a major theological problem inherent in Christian theology and also in other religious systems believing in incarnations (avatars) as well. Is it possible for that deity to be both human and divine and still be both absolutely powerful and absolutely good? In fact, that question also appears when we study a deity without an avatar.

This problem raises problematic concerns so vexing that it has its own name—*theodicy* (from Greek *theos-* "deity " and "*dike*" "order or right"), that is, the character of the deity or the "rightness" or "goodness" of the deity. Stated simply, the question is: How is it possible for a divinity to be all good and all-powerful or, using theological terms, *omnibenevolent* and *omnipotent*? Added to this could be another quality ascribed to God, *omniscience*, that is, having total knowledge, knowing everything that is, has been or will ever be. Are all these qualities possibly present in any deity whom a person might be moved to worship?

The problem is, these qualities contradict each other when placed in one entity. If God is an omnibenevolent and omnipotent creator, how is it possible for evil to exist? God's power and good would cancel out evil from existence.

Let's leave aside the question of omniscience for later.

Section One: Science and Theology as Dance Partners

Some religions, Zoroastrianism for example, confront the problem by having two natures possible within the same deity—a creative spirit making creation pure and an attacking spirit making it impure, either from outside or inside the deity.[14] Some even have two deities—one good, the other not.

If God is singular, then power or goodness have to be limited to explain the existence of evil. Christians have traditionally limited the omnipotence of God by providing humans free will, the right to defy and disobey God found in the Garden of Eden narrative in Genesis. Humans were damned with (or earned?) free will through "the fall" in Eden. Thus humans became capable of evil because of their freedom of choice, an exemption allowing the deity not to be evil. This theological position raises the concept of a self-limiting God, which results in many questions. For example, just how is such a deity limited? Is it completely limited, all the time or only sometimes? And if so, what is the extent of that limitation? Is God's limitation of evil restricted to only some persons of the deity or all? Is this limitation possible to overcome? If so, then how?

Of course, careful thought will reveal how this conundrum makes the Christian Incarnation very complex; granted, the Incarnation of a deity possibly might provide answers. There are, however, other theological solutions, many of which might give rise to heresies. No wonder the early church had heresies!

Another solution to the question of theodicy that is also possible is to limit God's good. Carl G. Jung, one of the fathers of psychotherapy, in *Answer to Job*[15] argues that it is possible for the deity to have limited omnibenevolence, that is, to be free of being all good all the time. This idea is thought by some as possibly Biblical; see these examples: Exodus 20:5; 34:14; Deuteronomy 4:23–24; 5:9; 6:15; 32:16; Joshua 24:19; Psalms 78:58; 79. There are also echoes in the New Testament in First Corinthians and in Matthew 21:12–13, and in Luke 19:45–46. Jung is not alone in suggesting such a possibility. Of course, careful thought will reveal how a deity capable of doing evil also makes the Christian Incarnation not only a solution, but also a problem. Perhaps a solution would be that God does not do evil; sometimes God just might do what *we think* is not good. How we think and how God thinks are surely different. That could be a blessing.

Does God Incarnate, the avatar, present human examples of goodness and also of evil? In the gospels, Jesus (Yeshua) becomes angry and forcefully cleanses the Temple in Jerusalem of the moneychangers and others, thus mirroring the concept of the angry jealous God in the Old Testament

The Dilemma of Theodicy

(Matthew 21:12; Mark 11:15–19; Luke 19:45–46; John 2:13–16). Yeshua also shows anger by condemning a fig tree (Luke 19:12–14). We seem to have examples in scripture that raise questions. Wouldn't it be unscriptural to say God does not get angry?

There seems to be a quandary in theodicy that is compounded further by the characteristic of *omniscience*, that is, all knowingness. Theologians and philosophers of religion have worried and argued over this quandary for centuries. It may be that there is a solution to the contradiction, but that has to come later in our discussion. For now, let's ask the simple question: Would you worship a deity who is going to allow a horrible plague in the next decade or another holocaust of a group of people, a group that includes you?

Some church leaders did opt for omniscience; for example, John Knox, the founder of Presbyterianism in Scotland, argued for predestination, as did St. Augustine of Hippo. Now that's a theological argument that's worth exploring further. The idea is that humans are predestined; they are either saved or damned for eternity. Does belief in such a deity, one who knows whose lives are predestined to be saved or to be damned, especially the latter when one doesn't know if one's fate is heaven or hell, does this belief motivate persons to become believers? Yes, if they are assured to be on the winning side, but is success truly guaranteed? Who really makes that guarantee? Can anyone really know the mind of God?

Those theologians who claim that they do know the mind of God are suspect at best, for a deity can change its mind, one of the consequences of being all powerful. God can change God's mind if God wants to; that power comes with omnipotence. Perhaps that's the answer to omniscience. God's ability to change decisions seems not to guarantee a person's predestination.

Is it possible that a human person is capable of knowing the mind of God? To claim so is truly a slippery slope; indeed in Knox's defense, there are Biblical passages that might allow a person to consider omniscience; for example—Jeremiah 29:11: "For I know the plans I have for you, says the Lord, plans for welfare and not for evil, to give you a future and a hope."

What this passage provides seems more of a declaration of benevolence than of omniscience. Careful reading yields the insight that the passage mentions *plans*. Plans are not outcomes, only hopes or aims, and when fulfilled, only then become outcomes. This passage might suggest omniscience, but that interpretation seems rather "stretched" at best, as do many of the others that also suggest omniscience. Are not God and every human being capable of a change of mind? So very much depends upon one's personal interpretation. One thing we learn from scripture is that God sometimes has changed God's mind.

Granted that a deity who already knows the outcome of your actions would have a very major sway over your life; that belief does motivate you to do what you are told are correct or good actions (and exactly who tells you this is most important). But are there not dilemmas that are not clear-cut enough or not unmistakably obvious regarding which choice to make? Such situations seem to arise in people's lives rather often, and those who are honest would admit that some choices they have made were wrong. Can't we do evil with the very best intentions? Life's lessons seem to say, surely, we can.

Unfortunately, human beings do not have omniscient minds, and to punish us for incorrect judgments would surely be cruel and unusual. Who would worship such a deity who made us the way we are and then punished us for not knowing the right answer?

Omniscience in a deity presents a multiplicity of problems for those who seek answers in their faith, particularly for those who look to a beneficent deity. Perhaps we should ask a more central theological question: Is it really necessary that God be omniscient? Perhaps it is not; on deity omniscience, we must wait for further insights and findings.

One should abhor proof texts, those selected verses from scripture that are used to win an argument but usually are used out of context. However, there is one interesting text for those who would tell us what is forthcoming from God's mind: Romans 11:33–34:

> O the depth of the riches and wisdom and knowledge of God! How unsearchable are His judgments and how inscrutable His ways. For who has known the mind of the Lord, or who has been His counselor? [See Isaiah 40:13–14 for comparison.]

Scientists probe the mysteries of God's creation, encountering mysteries needing solving, and propose theories which they hope to prove. In this way, scientists are also fathoming God's Creation and Mind.

CHAPTER 10

Science vs. Theology

Now THAT SCIENCE HAS been mentioned, we need to look at the long and sometimes bloody war between theology and science, particularly in the Western world. For many centuries, new ideas, including scientific ones, were frowned upon, often silenced, by the church, with a fervor sometimes leading to executions. The wars between science and religion have been going on even on up to our century; one has only to read about the strictures placed on Pierre Teilhard de Chardin SJ (1881–1955), an anthropologist and philosopher whose ideas were at first condemned. Only later were they allowed to be read while placed under caution; one had to read them very critically, remembering the church's objections about what he had written.

Teilhard de Chardin's ideas are broad on and represent an insightful rapprochement of science and theology, which this tome is also trying to do:

> He attempted to show that what is of permanent value in traditional philosophical thought can be maintained and even integrated with a modern scientific outlook if one accepts that the tendencies of material things are directed, either wholly or in part, beyond the things themselves toward the production of higher, more complex, more perfectly unified beings. Teilhard regarded basic trends in matter—gravitation, inertia, electromagnetism, and so on—as being ordered toward the production of progressively more complex types of aggregate. This process led to the increasingly complex entities of atoms, molecules, cells, and organisms, until finally the human body evolved, with a nervous

system sufficiently sophisticated to permit rational reflection, self-awareness, and moral responsibility.[16]

Teilhard de Chardin's belief was that the ultimate aim of evolution was to be found in the person of Jesus Christ. All of evolution was pointing to that goal for humans. Teilhard de Chardin's "rehabilitation" by the Catholic Church marks a pause in the war between church and science or perhaps only an armistice. Some non-Catholic Christian movements were earlier than the Catholic Church hierarchy in finding importance in scientific discoveries such as evolution; unfortunately, a few others still haven't and don't seem to be ready to do so.

Teilhard de Chardin is only one of many whose ideas were banned for religious reasons; some others were Galileo, Giordano Bruno, and Spinoza, and the list could go on for several pages. Some, such as Bruno, lost their lives; others suffered house arrest, as did Galileo, or social shunning as Spinoza. Bruno's fate of dying at the stake in an auto-da-fé was the fate of many other people. Please look up Giordano Bruno's scientific ideas; ahead of his time, he seemed to imply later scientific understanding.

It seems imprudent for theology to overlook the sciences, for they are the study of experimentally based ideas and theories with tested, verifiable results. Perhaps in seeking a new theology, we might find many new ideas by considering scientific discoveries important for our understanding theology.

We should turn to modern science for insight into some understanding of God. Creation itself should demonstrate qualities reflecting its Creator, as a pot has the mark of the potter's hands or a sculpture contains the vision and craft of who created it. Reality itself surely carries the mark of its Sculptor. Some of the mind-boggling concepts of the past two centuries have clustered around the fields of astronomy and physics; perhaps we can aim our search for a new theology (without slighting other scientific disciplines) at an understanding of some selected major breakthroughs in astrophysics and quantum mechanics. These exciting scientific fields, utilizing mathematics and observation to back their theoretical propositions (only later proven or disproven) offer sources for understanding how God might be better understood by studying the universe.

Science is not error proof; it is willing readily to admit its mistakes. Have those writing theology been as willing? How the universe works is surely relevant to discovering God's relationship to fragile human beings. As we shall see, there is, indeed, a great amount of scientific information. It requires careful study, but the possibility for gaining new theological insights should make that study worthwhile and possibly might provide breakthroughs in our understanding God.

Chapter 11

Science as a Good Source

WE NEED TO UNDERSTAND how science approaches belief, for that measured and careful stance is crucial to our grasp of how scientific discoveries might reinforce theology. Carlo Rovelli, an important theoretical physicist and author, gives a thoughtful presentation of how science approaches and understands truth. In his *Realty Is Not What It Seems: The Journey to Quantum Gravity*, Rovelli writes:

> This acute awareness of our ignorance is the heart of scientific thinking.
>
> ... To learn something, it is necessary to have the courage to accept that what we think we know, including our most rooted convictions, may be wrong, or at least naïve ... (259)

In a later paragraph, Rovelli observes:

> ... But if we are certain of nothing, how can we possibly rely on what science tells us? The answer is simple. Science is not reliable because it provides certainty. It is reliable because it provides us with the best answers we have at present. Science is the most we know so far about the problems confronting us. It is precisely its openness, its constant putting of current knowledge in question, that guarantees that the answers it offers are the best so far available; if you find better answers, these new answers become science.... (260)
>
> ... It's the awareness of our ignorance that gives science its reliability. And it is reliability that we need, not certainty ... The search for knowledge is not nourished by certainty; it is nourished by a radical distrust in certainty.

Science as a Good Source

> This means not giving credence to those who say they are in possession of the truth . . . (261)
>
> There is always . . . someone who pretends to tell us the ultimate answers. The world is full of people who say that they have The Truth, because they have got it from the fathers; they have read it a Great Book; they have received it directly from a god; they have found it in the depths of themselves. There is always someone who has the presumption to be the depository of Truth, neglecting to notice that the world is full of *other* depositories of Truth, each one with his own real Truth, different from that of the others. There is always some prophet dressed in white, uttering the words: 'Follow me, I am the true way.' (262)
>
> For my part, I prefer to look our ignorance in the face, accept it, and seek to look just a bit further: to try to understand that which we are able to understand. Not just because accepting this ignorance is the way to avoid being entangled in superstitions and prejudices, but because to accept our ignorance in the first place seems to me to be the truest, the most beautiful, and above all, the most honest way. (263)[17]

As so accurately detailed by physicist Rovelli, the method of science is to be preferred to that of belief that lacks careful examination and testing. Here arises a crucial question: Why has theology not allowed itself to study scientific methods as well as their conclusions, and why has it not incorporated them into an understanding of the divine? Why has theology, in most instances, not looked to the wonders of science as a source of insight into the divine? In seeking a new theology, shouldn't we turn to scientific inquiry and search out those insights regarding God's creation that such careful research might have discovered? How can we scientifically account for the escaping Hebrews crossing the Sea of Reeds (see Exodus 14:21–29 as well as the geography and hydrology of the Red [Reed] Sea); Joshua's adding time during a battle (which suggests insights into time and its relationship to space and gravity—Joshua 14:12–14.); Isaiah's demonstration against the priests of Baal (which implies applications of combustible chemistry; 1 Kings 18:20–39); Daniel's calming presence in the lion's den (that takes us into nonhuman psychobiology; Daniel 6:14–24), and many of the other fascinating events recorded in Hebrew, Christian, Islamic and almost all sacred writings.

Some such narratives as those above could be seen as lacking mystery, especially when compared to the multiple actions and intriguing structure of a black hole or the destructive explosion of a nova, the shattering of colliding galaxies or the birthing of new stars or the beginning of time itself. We could include many other phenomena being studied across the spectrum of the sciences. The truth in this historical standoff seems obvious: *science is not anathema to theology unless theology makes it so.*

Given quantum mechanics, seeking what is possible—the sea of energy that constitutes the universe, or the expulsion of photons and neutrino, or the information shared between elements to create new matter and all the other phenomena available to all scientists including mathematicians—all are exciting and also relevant to theology. Seeking what lies within or possibly beyond the quantum field or what constitutes the initiation of the composition of a photon or many other scientific phenomena are worth pondering by theologians. We are beginning to understand the methods and materials used by the Creator of this universe, and we are just beginning slowly to formally and mathematically understand. Science is too rich a resource to be avoided by theologians. We must open our beliefs to scientific discoveries which can demonstrate the Creator's plan.

Chapter 12

Where We Are in the Universe

LET'S TAKE A LOOK scientifically at where we are in the universe, at the furthermost we can perceive when seeking those ultimate limits—both outward and inward—of what we know. Let's start outward.

Scientists use an exponential scale when writing large numbers; this scale lists a base number and then adds numbers to set the larger number. For example, $a^1 = a$; however, a^2 *is a multiplied by a*; thus the addition of a superscript to a numeral is an instruction to multiply it by the number of times listed in the superscript; thus, $10^2 = 100$; $10^3 = 1{,}000$. This will be helpful when we start measuring distances in the universe, both out and in, that is, both to the farthest exteriors of the universe and tiniest interiors of known being.

Astronomers's scales use light years—how far light travels in a year; the speed of light is 186,282 miles per second. Scientists prefer meters, which are used more universally. According to Caleb Scharf and Ron Miller's "The Observable Universe,"[18] the radius of the observable universe is somewhat beyond 10^{27}. The superscripts can either be plus, 10^3 meters, or minus 10^{-3}, which is one thousandth ($10 \times 10 \times 10$) of a meter. According to Scharf and Miller, human experience, what we can see unaided, begins at 10^{-3} on the lower side to the other end of our unaided experiential range at 10^3, somewhat above a few kilometers without mechanical aids. Objects similar to planets go from "hundreds of kilometers in diameter to well over 100,000 kilometers" while stars have diameters of around 10^{10} with the smallest about 10^8 meters, smaller than our Sun at 10^9 while the largest stars reach sizes of more than 10^{11}.

Section One: Science and Theology as Dance Partners

Our own galaxy seems rather skimpy with only some two billion stars; the smaller galaxies such as our own have only a few billion, but the larger galaxies may contain trillions of stars, according to Scharf and Miller.

Going back to the span of the human unaided experiential spectrum, we see how using light years helps us grasp these distances. Light covers the distance of one meter at 3.3 nanoseconds (10^{-19}), and it takes only 500 seconds for light to travel from the Sun to the Earth. It takes 100 quadrillion seconds for light to travel to us from the cosmic horizon (10^{27}). We need to remember that light's speed is 186,282 miles per second. An average human life lasts about 2.5 billion seconds (10^9) according to Scharf and Miller. Only recently have astronomers been glimpsing activities taking place near the edge of the universe. "What has been seen is very exciting; for example, the discovery of a cosmic megamerger that made the news (Aug. 8, 2017) and was reported BBC and *Nature*:

> It is a cosmic pileup in the far reaches of the universe and nothing like it has ever been seen before. Using the most powerful telescopes on Earth, astronomers have spotted 14 burning-hot galaxies hurtling toward each other on an inevitable galactic collision course at the edge of the observable universe.
>
> Computer models show that when these galaxies do collide, they will form the core of a colossal galaxy cluster so large that it will be the most massive known in the cosmos.
>
> This chaotic, energy-filled region, described . . . in *Nature*, is called a protocluster, and researchers say it is more active than any section of the universe that they have ever observed. 'There are huge energetics involved, like 10,000 supernova going off at a time,' said Scott Chapman, a physicist at Dalhousie University in Halifax, Canada, who worked on the study.
>
> As if all that wasn't crazy enough, the authors said that 14 galaxies are known as 'starburst galaxies,' which means stars are forming at a furious rate. The research team estimates that they 'could be making stars as much as 10,000 times faster than the Milky Way.' And they are all crammed into a space 'just three times the size of our own galaxy. In addition, the whole system is located 90 percent of the way to the edge of the observable universe.'[19]

Just now, we are seeing and learning about major events in the universe whose light takes over 12.4 light-years to reach us. These events, near the edge of the observable universe, are far larger, immensely more complex, and perhaps far more shattering than any humans have known or surmised.

Science is discovering more information than ever before, and that information is on a scale far beyond what we had ever previously comprehended.

So then, what does this very huge universe have to do with theology?

First, these distances show how very small we as a species are on our isolated third planet in a moribund solar system around a single average star on an outlying arm of our galaxy, the Milky Way.

Second, these measurements show how insignificant we could be in this universe, which we believe has been created by what we tend to call God.

Third, these observations demonstrate how expansive and powerful that deity is, if that God did create our universe as theology assumes. Our minds, reaching towards God, have problems grasping just how powerful, wondrous, and even beyond our imaginations God might be. That awe should not stop us from trying to understand God's wonders. On the contrary, is that not exactly the task that theology sets for itself? Is it not to help us to see God's wonders and power?

Robert Browning captured the task of the theologian well in one of his most famous poems, *Andrea del Sarto*:

> Ah, but a man's reach should exceed his grasp,
> Or what's a heaven for? . . . (Lines 97–98a)

Theology needs to extend its *reach* so that it may *grasp* more.

Chapter 13

Looking Down Inside Creation

Having gone out to the edge of the observable universal horizon (10^{27}), we now might venture into the world of the miniature. According to Scharf and Miller, "The Observable Universe," the midpoint between the outer range of our observation and the inner range, 10^{-4}, is just beyond our unaided experiential spectrum (10^3 to 10^{-3}). Following their comments further, we see that viruses, the smallest entities that resemble life, are to be found at 10^{-7}; atoms are at 10^{-10} and the proton, a part of the nucleus of an atom, at 10^{-15}. Making up the parts of the elements of the atoms are the quarks; they reside at 10^{-20}.[20] The smallest portion of energy is the quantum, discovered and named by Max Plank, who theorized that the electromagnetic field was made up of energy packets—quanta, the size of these packets depending upon the frequency of their electromagnetic waves. He worked out that for every type of this energy packet, a quantum, there was a frequency; from this, he began the study of quantum mechanics by positing Plank's Constant, E (energy) = $\hbar$ (a quantum) at v (a specific frequency). The formula for Planck's Constant is $E = \hbar v$[21] showing that energy could be divided (*quantified*, ergo *quantum*) into energy units.

Scharf and Miller posit Plank's Constant at 10^{-35}, the smallest unit yet discovered. They noted: "There are as many orders of magnitude in scale from there [Planck's Constant] to a speck of dirt as from a speck of dirt to the entire observable universe."[22]

That brings us to the limit of how small we can go. If you are feeling huge finding out how small things can become, you should consider that

Looking Down Inside Creation

"our bodies are not wholly our own, because they also serve as Darwinian battlefields for trillions of bacteria and viruses."[23] Have you ever wondered how those entities might regard their "battlefields" were they to have consciousness (which evidently they do not)? Would these bacteria or viruses then regard us as deities? How might they theorize in their theology (if they had one) about your morning shower?

Where we are in our universe, that is, from 10^{-35} (smallest) to 10^{27} (largest), reinforces our sense of smallness and insignificance, but also projects a sense of awe when we conceptualize a deity capable of creating something so vast, from greatest to tiniest, and also so wondrous. This scientific perspective reinforces our need for a new theology to appreciate our interesting location in God's creation.

CHAPTER 14

Using Einstein's Discoveries

So why not give science a try? Why not begin with one of the most creative minds of the 20th century—Alfred Einstein (1889-1952)? I love that picture of the world-renown genius sticking out his tongue. Interestingly, I've never seen any pictures of theologians doing so. Are scientists more likely to take themselves less seriously than theologians?

Newton and classical physicists thought of gravity as the force of a larger object pulling on a smaller object; for example, the Sun pulling on the Earth, the Earth pulling on the Moon, etc. For Newton, space itself was empty or filled with *ether*, whatever that was. Gravity for Newton was the force of a larger object attracting a smaller object, like a magnet. Relative size seemed to matter.

These ideas began to lose sway with the discoveries of Faraday and Maxwell as well as others studying the electromagnetic field. What we call space vibrates and even oscillates, expands and contracts, but what is it?

Einstein didn't believe Newton's concepts were accurate. Instead of space being empty or filled with *ether*, space was filled with something and it was not Newton's *ether*. Einstein did not climb on the quantum bandwagon at first, but he did later when evidence became convincing. When looking for what space was filled with, Einstein's answer was *gravity*. He postulated that gravity and space are the same, and his theory has been widely proven. Gravity is part of a field filling space. Einstein theorized and other scientists later proved that space and gravity are combined. Instead of being a force analogous to a string on a yoyo (as Newton viewed it), gravity was similar to one of those games in which you drop a penny into an ever-tightening funnel and the coin spins around and around prior to slowly falling into the dark resembling a mechanical black hole.

An image of gravity as a force. "Gravity Probe B and Space–Time," NASA.

Imagine, if you will, that you hold a bed sheet with three other friends, each grasping a corner. Now you put a basketball in the center of the sheet; it represents the Sun. A curved field of space appears on the sheet. Now rapidly spin a marble (representing the Earth) around the space depressed by the ball. You see the marble circle the basketball just as Earth circles the Sun. Gravity and space react the same; the basketball curves the sheet as the Sun curves the space of the solar system. Were your marble fast enough, it would continue to circle.

Now, what might space–gravity have to do with other previously thought-to-be separate concepts that seem divergent but are the same when scientifically examined? If we earlier imagined that space and gravity were separate when they were the same, then can two theological concepts possibly be related in the same way, for instance, God's power (omnipotence) and God's goodness (omnibenevolence)? Although they seem separate, are they really?

A central conundrum of theology is the problem of deity or deities being both omnibenevolent and omnipotent; these traits, when shared by the same deity, create the problem of *theodicy*, which asks how these two qualities can logically coexist. Let's leave, for now, the question of *omniscience*, that is, the deity knowing what has happened, is happening and what will happen.

Einstein melded these two supposed differing concepts—space and gravity—and that meld, in time, convinced physicists. Following that example, let's propose that divine omnibenevolence and omnipotence are just as identical as are gravity/space.

This proposition argues that one can't accomplish aims that are good without some kind of power to reach that good, and that one can't exercise power to accomplish aims that are lasting without attempting to do, at the same time, that which is good. Therein possibly resides the power of non-violent action, of effective organizing and acting without hate and spite, for if there is hate and/or spite, one is not working towards the good. The method influences the goal and vice versa, a process that resembles closely a physics particle field. There is what many mistakenly call power, and then there is real, effective, lasting power. We humans might learn from these historical lessons such as non-violent actions. In science, we shall see that scrutiny changes outcomes; in good works, motive for good and not evil operates the same way.

Nonviolent action, to be truly effective, seems to demand forgiveness, just as Jesus (Yeshua) demonstrated on the cross. The effect of the Crucifixion over time was to motivate Yeshua's followers to spread their newfound beliefs around the world. Perhaps it is this type of action for which humans were given the ability to wield non-violent power and even gain the knowledge of what is good and what is not. Graham Greene puts this idea convincingly in his powerful and insightful novel, *The Power and the Glory*. Notice in the novel the parallels to the Crucifixion.

At a historical first glance, the Crucifixion of Jesus (Yeshua) and two thieves looks much as any other Roman execution, one of so very many across the Roman Empire; note the high number of crucifixions following the Spartacus slave and gladiator rebellion. However, Christian theologians would argue that the power generated by that one execution and its aftermath in history is highly effective and affective, primarily proven by the spread of Christian beliefs and ideas around the globe. Christianity grew out of a people living in Judea, which had recently suffered from violent uprisings and revolutions, those of the Maccabees and then the Jews in answer to the conquest by the Romans. Rome used military violence to accomplish political and spiritual goals. Yet the nonviolence of the cross, offering forgiveness to the killers, allowed good to triumph and gain power around the world, where power alone used in revolts and conquests had dismally failed. Thus the good and power, when united, were effective and lasting where neither separately had triumphed until effectively combined. They are a field, similar to gravity/space and other fields in physics.

Can raw power without good intention and non-evil actions prevail in the long run? Careful study of history shows that power alone does not long preserve what it attempts. On the other hand, can doing good accomplish any lasting goal except self-congratulation if performed without actions that utilize at least a modicum of power? Our attempting to do good without utilizing non-violent power for change seems to alter little if anything. Power without seeking to do the good seems spurious, empty, and futile. It is also dangerously self-aggrandizing. So also is the attempt to do good if it lacks power.

Feeding the starving accomplishes little until you work to provide food for the rest of the year. This reasoning is why some believers negatively react to free Thanksgiving meals for the needy; the hungry need food all year long. The little old lady helped to cross the busy street has more streets to cross, and must do so in coming days. We can use this idea of power and goodness as one insight—similar to that of gravity/space—to the study of politics and wars.

Examine the following photograph of an old starved Jew, awaiting execution beside a trench where his fellow Vinnitza villagers's bodies were tossed after their deaths. Doing these murders of Jews is an *Einstazgruppen*, a Nazi extermination squad, its designated task to wipe out as many Jews as possible in Nazi conquered territories; however, as adept as such Nazis were at murder, their goal, killing all Jews and undesirables, was never reached (Thank God!) and they failed, even given multiple opportunities. The Holocaust, mass killings along with concentration and death camps, although horrifying, did fail; some Jews survived and once again had a homeland. An undoubted power was thwarted and ended.

The Nazi mission was a guaranteed failure because they did not have the other part of power, the action to achieve the good. Granted, millions died, but the thousand–year Reich only lasted about twelve years.

Section One: Science and Theology as Dance Partners

Last Jew in Vinnitza

Another photograph from World War II might help us see a victums's calmness clearly; a Ukrainian boy has just seen his family murdered by an Nazi death squad. He stands calmly, possibly having a similar insight as the old Jew.

Using Einstein's Discoveries

Ukrainian boy faces death, United States Holocaust Museum

The Nazi executioners had thought themselves powerful, but were they really? Notice the villager standing at the left in the photo; he seems to ignore the calm courage of the young martyr and lack a sense of the moment. In this scene, is there any doubt regarding which person demonstrates true moral courage? The good without power may suffer, but the good, empowered, often does less so.

Power without benevolence, as seen in these photos, is empty, atrocious, at best self-aggrandizing, for those exercising it ,and over time, futile and ineffective in accomplishing the desired goals. The Nazis lost the war. The Third Reich didn't last a thousand years. After almost 14 years, all that remained was a great suffering, ashes, maimed and soul-shattered forlorn humans wandering in ruins.

Goodness lacking power seems just as ineffective, possibly wasteful of labor, and very similar to power lacking the good. Such goodness may also be self-aggrandizing. Good and power seem to operate as the same entity in order to accomplish lasting change and human benefit. Is not the unity of good and power the source of the power of nonviolence?

Gravity and space constitute a single field that was not, in the past, recognized as the same, but through scientific investigation, we can now understand gravity/space as being the same. This connection suggests that careful uses of power, united with thoughtful, conscientious application of good, are one.

Section One: Science and Theology as Dance Partners

Science has provided the examples of "thought experiments" *(Gedankenexperiments)* from history that we can use in our understanding of theodicy. This pairing (good/power) may be analogous or not, but it is this kind of linking of seemingly disparate concepts that demonstrates why theology should be open to science's new insights and methods. Such a linking as the good and power might prove in time to be mistaken, like any proposed scientific or theological finding, but it does stretch us to examine new concepts and discover the new.

We need to introduce into our theological minds much more of these brain-stretching *Gedankenexperiments*. Thought experiments are surely not unknown in theology; we just seem to be somewhat more hesitant to practice them.

CHAPTER 15

It's About Time, and So is God

CARLO ROVELLI IN HIS *Reality is Not What It Seems: The Journey to Quantum Gravity* warns us:

> No, quantum mechanics is more than granularity... And there is the fact that what matters is not how things *are*, but rather how they *interact*.
>
> At an extremely small scale, space is a fluctuating swarm of quanta that act upon one another, and together act upon things, manifesting themselves in these interactions as spin networks: grains [bits of energy] interrelated with one another....
>
> Physical space is the fabric resulting from the ceaseless swarming of this web of relations. The... [quanta]... are not in a place but rather create places through their interactions. Space is created by the interaction of individual quanta of gravity.
>
> We have already seen that Einstein demonstrated that gravity and space were united. Space twists, undulates; it curves; it has been argued by physicists that it might be in miniscule tubes or strings or loops, depending upon their theories. It is the "stuff" of quantum interactions and these make possible the curves of space, sometimes carrying the bending of light (photons) around a star because of that star's gravity.[24]

Carl Friedrich Gauss, the discoverer of the Gaussian curve in mathematics, had a student, Bernhard Riemann, whose dissertation was about the properties of curved space. Riemann's mathematical equation is known as *Riemann's Curvature*, indicated in astrophysical equations by the letter *R*. Space does curve and so does time, because it is the same thing, *space/time/gravity*.[25]

Einstein with his theory of general relativity not only melded gravity and space into *space*; he also melded space and time into *space/time*. In a laboratory with atomic clocks that can measure time to infinitesimally short lengths, if you put one of these highly accurate atomic clocks on the basement floor and another on the roof several stories above, after a day or so the lower clock would be slightly slower than the one on the roof.[26]

This experiment shows that time is elastic because it is one and the same as gravity/space. Astronauts in space flight do age slower than those on the ground, demonstrating that time changes with gravitational changes. Such changes might seem miniscule, but if placed on a galactic or universal scale, they loom much larger. The joke is that living on a mountain lets you live longer.[27]

How does this have relevancy for theology? One of the time change events in the Bible that stands out is in Judges 10:12–14, where Joshua's army was defeating an enemy army in the south of the Promised Land, aided by a hailstorm that killed more enemy soldiers than did the Israelite army. Joshua prayed that the day would last longer in order to complete the victory. The passage in Judges 10 states that the day was lengthened. Was space/time involved? Possibly, we don't know for sure, but it is a possibility. Science could give us insights into such phenomena if they did occur as recorded.

A similar phenomenon might have happened in the last century. According to Damien F. Mackey, similar was the Great Solar Miracle at Fatima, October 10, 1917. Mackey writes that thousands of persons in the Fatima area of Portugal witnessed that the Sun swirled and stopped and then swirled again; time seemed to be prolonged. Being careful scientifically, we need to investigate both of these phenomena, Joshua's and that at Fatima. Even though photographs taken at Fatima are rather poor, researchers have found that the sightings could have been sundogs, reflections of the sun on each side of the sky that can seem to waver with the air rippling on a very hot or cold day.[28] Despite the belief of the crowds at Fatima, there is good evidence to doubt this "miracle."[29]

Knowing what we do now from astronomy and physics, particularly about waves in the quanta space/gravity/time field, it seems that larger waves of quanta carrying photons might account for some such phenomena, provided they actually occurred. The Fatima event does have some photographic evidence, but there is no scientific proof that Joshua's time

It's About Time, and So is God

elongation or the Fatima event occurred as warps of time/space. Given today's theories of time, even provided the necessary forces were actively present, there still remains cause for doubt.

Please notice that a commonly overlooked aspect of miracles is not necessarily the nature of the events but their *timing*. The miraculous is not necessarily only what happened. Included in the equation of the event is the crucial *when* and *where*, the right time and place. We should notice these factors in viewing miracles, for the time of the event is a crucial factor. Our asking *how* sometimes gets in the way of our understanding the *when*.

Let's look at one example, the wedding at Cana (John 2: 1–11). The miracle takes place after almost all of the wine has been consumed. The catering steward confronts the bridegroom about serving the best wine last. According to John's gospel, the wedding at Cana was the first of Yeshua's miracles. Was its purpose to show Jesus's divinity? Did the new wine taste better because the guests had already drunk multiple toasts? Was there a hidden store of wine being saved for later occasions? Both explanations deny the miracle; however, the important point is that the miracle occurred only *after* all the purchased wine was supposedly gone. Was the miracle performed so a bridegroom wouldn't be embarrassed? Not a very good reason to do a miracle, is it? What else could point to divine intervention? Time does indeed matter, and *when* something happens can possibly be the most important element from a theological perspective.

Science helps us realize how important time is when viewing miracles. A scientist studies not only *what* happens but *when* and *how* and, most importantly, *why*. Would not these guidelines improve our grappling theologically with the stories of miraculous events in the sacred texts of religions? Thinking adults should welcome some close scrutiny of supposedly miraculous tales. Perhaps we need to realize that sometimes the questionable elements in our sacred stories, just as in the lives of the saints, need to be closely examined and very carefully studied.

Chapter 16

One of Science's Uncivil Battles

As we saw earlier, the Church seemed to wage war against science for several centuries, forcing scientists to toe the line of orthodoxy in the then current theological thought or else face consequences, as did Galileo, Giordano Bruno, Boethius, Michael Servetus, Hypatia, Antoine Lavoisier, Roger Bacon, Cecco d'Ascoli, Étienne Dolet, Pomponio Algerio, Lucilio Vanini and many other theologians, scientists and mathematicians.

In all fairness, we need to observe that scientists themselves have not had a spotless history of combating ideas with which they disagreed. One modern example of how such a quarrel can happen, even to those who seek to have open minds regarding facts, is the following. At least, no scholars were wantonly killed.

When Werner Heisenberg announced his uncertainty or indeterminacy principle, that is, "the more precisely the position [of an electron or other atomic element] is determined, the less precisely the momentum is known, and conversely,"[30] it became evident that: ". . . It is therefore not possible to make a measurement without disturbing the object under study in an essential, unpredictable way. . . . [Q]uantum mechanics places fundamental limits on what is *measurable* and it is impossible to do anything other than speculate on what is not measurable."[31]

Heisenberg noted that the law of causality itself was flawed:

> Physics ought to describe only the correlation of observations. One can express the true state of affairs better in this way: Because all experiments are subject to the laws of quantum mechanics . . .

it follows that quantum mechanics established the final failure of causality.[32]

These concepts were applied to the quandary of whether space/time was a field or consisted of particles. Niels Bohr saw that in some experiments it was possible to regard electrons as waves and in others as particles. He felt it was not possible to devise an experiment to demonstrate the behavior of both types [wave and particle] simultaneously. He realized that some scientists could ask questions regarding quanta's wave-like and others its particle-like properties; therefore, it was "pointless to enquire about the 'true' nature of quantum reality, as this is something we can never know."[33]

Bohr's solution was *complementarity*, that is, they were both wave and particle. In presenting his complementarity position, Bohr was in essence stating that science had a marked limitation on the ability of scientists to acquire scientific knowledge. This became known as the Copenhagen interpretation, which set up limitations on what experiments could prove since many events were not observable but limited to the instruments made to create them.[34] This position then became a problem in the investigation of quantum theory. Quanta were not observable, therefore, supposedly outside the range of science.

A parallel stance in philosophy, arising from suggestions by David Hume, amplified by Auguste Comte, and formalized by Ernst Mach, was established earlier. Mach, representing the group, argued: "We should not attach a deeper significance to the concepts used in theory or the conceptual entities they describe if these are not in themselves observable."[35]

In Vienna, a new group of thinkers including Moritz Schlink, Rudolph Carnap and Otto Neurath worked on these ideas in fashioning Logical Positivism. With one stroke, the Logical Positivists eliminated from philosophy centuries of "pseudo-statements" about mind, being, reality and God. This threw theology out the window. The views of the Vienna Circle continued to challenge the philosophy of science past the middle of the twentieth century.[36] Fortunately, this argument continuing into middle of the twentieth century is rapidly dying out.

A statement credited to Niels Bohr at this time was: "There is no quantum world. There is only an abstract quantum physical description. It is wrong to think that the task of physics is to find out *how* nature is. Physics concerns *what we can say* about nature."[37] In that one comment, Niels Bohn had denied the validity of understanding quantum mechanics. Some scholars seemed to have philosophically shot themselves in the foot. Logical Positivism denies much of scientific study. For these thinkers, theology would be only idle speculation.

Logical Positivism limits scientific research and keeps it captive to the limitations of our senses. Claiming logicality, it in fact completely denies mathematics. How do you possibly observe the square root of minus one ($\sqrt{-1}$) or ($-1 + -1 = +1$), the addition of negative numbers yielding a positive? A Logical Positivist would be unable to explain or do the math. Research on the atomic level was then beyond sensory grasp, but these ideas were ignored for obvious reasons. The influence of Logical Positivism began to evaporate in science rather quickly. Logical Positivism demonstrates how intellectual brainstorms can sweep through some scholarly groups as fads tend do in other social groups.

CHAPTER 17

Some Solutions about Quanta

BOHR AND THE COPENHAGEN Circle had seemed to assert that the quantum level of reality was unknowable, which seemed to mean that what causes causality is not causal or even understandable. The quanta posited by Planck's Constant were deduced but not observed, theorized but not proven, because they lacked actual sensory representation. Their effect was observed, but not the entities, the quanta themselves. The meeting of physicists at Lake Como in September 1927 was contentious and influenced by the Copenhagen Circle with what became Logical Positivism.[38]

Two months later, at the Fifth Solvay Conference in Brussels, "the founders of quantum theory—Planck, Einstein, Bohr, de Broglie—and the new generation of quantum *mechanics*—Born, Heisenberg, Pauli, Schrödinger, Dirac—were all to be in attendance."[39] There, de Broglie interpreted wave vs. particle from a different perspective; it wasn't wave *or* particle, it was a wave *realized* as particles.[40]

Why this new interpretation was necessary seems today confusing, for if there were a wave, it had to have some constituents, that is, particles, and there was no reason why particles could not constitute a wave, as drops of water do. An aspect of this idea was given by Einstein through his "thought" experiments (*Gedankenexperiments*), primarily building on the effects seen when light is projected through two slits, where it can be seen that the expected result is that the photons seem to "select" which slit to pass through. There are only two lines of light; however on the receptor, there are several more lines. This seemed to prove that there were waves of photons (light) experienced as particles.[41]

Consequently, Bohr began to reexamine his theoretical position on the complementarity.[42] It was becoming apparent that in quantum theory, quanta constitute a wave that could only be "realized" as particles.[43] The problem still existed that quanta could not be directly observed, but at that time neither could molecules or atoms.

Decades later, electron microscopes would allow scientists to view molecules and today even larger atoms. After Hiroshima and Nagasaki in 1945, there could be no doubt atoms existed; however, the quantum level still remains beyond sensory observation, although there could be little doubt that it exists (as seen in the effects of interstellar spectaculars).

What might provide insights for theology in the debate about whether quanta are particles or waves seems obvious. Even though he hadn't adopted the theory of quantum mechanics completely and may have had some doubts about its nature, Einstein was able with his thought experiments to cause others to see the questions from a different perspective. He kept these theories and their theorists on the right tract. Theological discussion would benefit from such interventions and conferences as well, and, frankly, one would hope such occur more often. There is need for new concepts and ideas in theology, and for thinkers to reach out for *new* theories about how we might understand the divine creating something new every day. More interdenominational and interfaith conferences are needed.

If physicists and other scientists can hammer out new concepts and gain new insights, even though sometimes contentiously while being open to other arguments, why cannot theologians from different faith backgrounds and differing religious persuasions do likewise? Do we not believe in peace and mutual respect? Do not the sacred needs of theological exploration demand our dedicated working with ideas outside of our familiar beliefs and institutional backgrounds?

Chapter 18

Regarding Absolutes

In eastern North Carolina, a short shower had made the highway slick. A car rounded a curve under the speed limit, hit the slick pavement, then slid and tumbled, crashing. Inside, the young man driving was killed instantly, leaving his widowed mother and younger sister to mourn.

We'll return to this situation when we have more insights that might help us put it in perspective. That perspective has to do with the question of absolutes. Scientists several decades ago regarded the speed of light, 186,282 miles per second, as the absolute fastest anything could travel in the universe. Something was faster and that something was the velocity of energy expressed in the quanta jumps, as de Broglie had predicted. In physics, light speed had been crowned as the fastest anything could travel, the *absolute*, but not anymore.

About a collision of neutron stars (observed Aug. 17, 2017), Eric Betz noted: "Their collision was fast and violent, likely spawning a black hole. And a shudder—a gravitational wave—rippled across the fabric of space-time. The light from it followed seconds later." [44]

Amazingly, astronomers can now detect these ripples in space/time at the Laser Interferometer Gravitational Wave Observatory (LIGO), which made the Nobel-winning discovery of gravitational waves for the first time in 2015.[45]

Section One: Science and Theology as Dance Partners

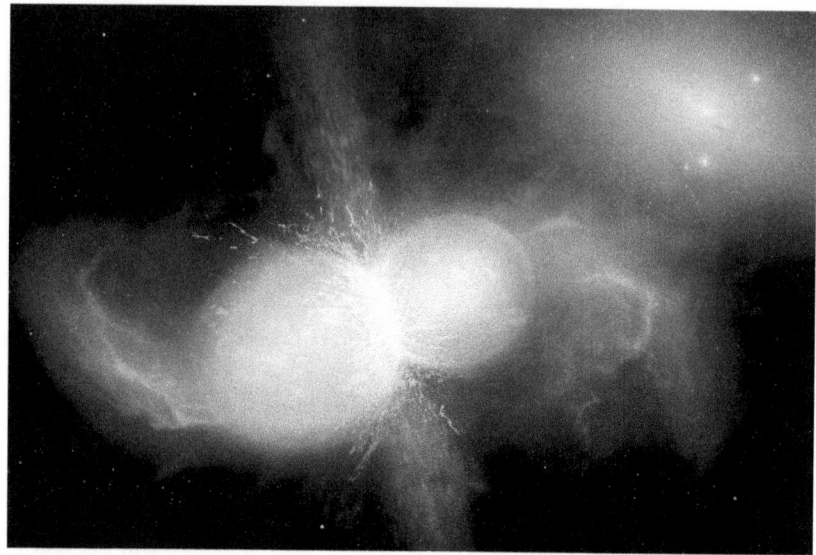

Two Neutron stars colliding; Eso1733s University of Warwick/Mark Garlick, Wikipedia

If the 2017 gravity ripple in space-time preceded the arrival of the light, then its speed was faster than the speed of light. The meaning of this event is important, for it signifies that one of science's major absolutes was no longer valid. The speed of light was no longer the fastest in the universe. One of science's major absolutes had been brought to a halt? We seriously need to ask: Are there really any absolutes? This is a major question for science and for theology.

These scientific events raise an interesting question. What would a theology look like in a universe with no absolutes or perhaps with only one absolute—a lone deity we call God?

Now, let's return to eastern North Carolina and the grieving mother. Several years later, an interim pastor had preached a sermon on the power of God. The dead youth's mother asked the pastor to visit that afternoon, and there she asked a very difficult question often asked by parents: "Why did God allow my son to die?" Too often many clergy have been faced with the same question. Given a theology without absolutes, one possible answer would be that God was not present (non-omnipresence). Another answer might be that a person's death, no matter how we might wish it to have meaning, sometimes doesn't have any that we understand. There remain many answers given a universe without absolutes.

Regarding Absolutes

Combat in war presents example after example of seemingly random death. In a world seeming to lack absolutes, new, more insightful theological answers have to be given to those asking this question. A new theology should seek to present answers to such lingering questions. This is only one of a clustering of conundrums that cause people constantly to search, time after time, for answers, and in our present theology, they are finding few if any.

If asked what a world lacking absolutes would be like, I can only say, "Perhaps it looks a lot like the one we live in now." Were I able to create an absolute—no mortal is so able, but we can wish—it would be that no parent should be forced to bury a beloved child.

There may be no absolutes in this world, and such seems a difficult world in which to reconstruct our theology. At this point, theology runs into what seems an impenetrable wall. It must be carefully examined and, if possible, penetrated.

Our religious institutions can no longer expect the old answers to be sufficient. We need to grasp every idea available, searching every branch of knowledge—including science, which we too often ignore—that could help us in our search for a new theology. There can be no doubt that all sciences offer many special insights that are well worth investigating. Is it not also possible that we might gain major understanding about God as a Master Builder by studying sciences which spend time trying to understand just what is out there in our universe, what it is made of? The possibility is we might answer our questions regarding the ultimate conundrums: Why was the universe made? Why are we here? What is the meaning of life and death? What constitutes a meaningful life?

CHAPTER 19

Regarding Constants

IN POSITING HIS LAWS of motion in the *Philosophiæ Naturalis Principia Mathematica* (1687), known as the *Principia*, Isaac Newton fashioned his second law as: $F = ma$ where *force* (f) when applied to an object's *mass* (m) creates an *acceleration* (a) or movement. The mass (m), the constant of the equation, changes without adding any more material. However, there are two masses, that is, an object can have a mass that doesn't change (supporting Newton's equation) or one that does change. You can add more mass because as an object accelerates, the resistance to the speeding up increases, and that increase throws Newton's equation off, for the object's mass also increases. Thus, there is a difficulty in calculating the forces at work; a fixed mass had been the constant in Newton's equation. What was needed was a *gravitational constant*, known as "the big G." In 1798, Henry Cavendish was able to measure an approximate "big G" but not accurately. Later, Hungarian scientist Loránd Eötvös made insightful improvements, then Jens H. Gundlach and Stephen M. Merkowitz were able to read a finding with additional numbers for big G; their total was measured at .000000000066742, a weak gravity constant, a bacterium's weight.[46]

What these examples demonstrate is that science is dependent upon experiments that change and improve investigators's findings. Sometimes, scientists recognize it is impossible as yet to measure accurately some physical properties. Over time, more accurate information may be found. This constant improvement is central to science, and thus scientific theories can be adjusted and changed if needed.

Regarding Constants

Werner Heisenberg, for example, proposed his celebrated "uncertainty principle" which helps explain the impossibilities of absolutely precise measurements. Formulated in 1927, Heisenberg noted that variable properties appear in pairs, such as location/speed or energy/time; these pairs do not allow the *exact* measurement of the other member of the pair. Measurement is blocked.

What were once regarded as constants in the universe are subject to change. Scientists still search to find constants than hold for all of time/space. in 1938, English physicist Paul Dirac proposed that Newton's "G" (Universal Gravity Constant), then regarded as a major constant, might decrease as the universe ages. Neil De Grasse Tyson noted: "Today there's practically a cottage industry of physicists desperately seeking fickle constants."[47] It means there might be no constants in our universe, just as there are no absolutes; however, there still remains the Hubble Constant, the rate of expansion of the universe, and it is still under contention.

It seems that theology has a great need to invite scientists to come to their dance floor and help them enjoy a better partnership. The impact that science can have on theology, if the scholars of belief are willing, could be enormous. Scientific findings, which are multiplying rapidly today, would allow those interested in the central questions of faith and God to reach new and perhaps more meaningful insights, and also to discover how belief can be underscored by known facts rather than merely supposition. In our seeking such a new theology, we surely must allow scientists to join our conversations so that we, if necessary, may reevaluate our knowledge and beliefs.

This is not an argument that persons aiming to become clergy or theologically trained should all also become theoretical physicists. That stupid idea was "shot down" by none other than Stephen Hawking: "To do research on the fundamental laws that govern the universe would require a commitment of time that most people don't have; the world would soon grind to a halt if we all tried to do theoretical physics."[48] But we should ask seminarians to become familiar with basic scientific concepts; we also might ask scientists to aid us all in making their discoveries more transparent and relevant to twenty–first century minds attempting to wrestle with theological enigmas.

SECTION TWO

Questions About Avatars— Gods Who Become Human

A CAREFUL STUDY OF the possibilities for avatars in major world religions yields those problems incorporated in the avatar of Christianity with its incarnated God.

This single human/god (avatar) creates both scientific and theological questions. A brief survey of major world religions provides you, the reader, a perspective for viewing how the Christ event raises major questions, such as: its timing and locale, the question of gender, the ethnic identification, religious activity and the competition, as well as the questions of how divine and/or human is our avatar. Reasons for having an Incarnation are discussed and some interpretations of those findings clarify the comparisons in the section.

CHAPTER 20

Human Deities or Avatars

AN *AVATAR* IS A deity that has become incarnated, that is, taken on a form found in natural creation—a deity becomes human. In essence, an avatar is a deity which is substantial matter that can be sensed by humans.

There are many believed-in avatars in the world's religions. The first religions, *animism,* were filled with beliefs projected on natural creatures, objects, phenomena or forces of nature seen as divine. Parsing some major modern religions for avatars and searching for parallel theologies, we might discover that they have few avatars, if any, or many more than one. Christianity has only one—*Christ*, meaning "the anointed one."

First, we might look at a modern religion that seems to be non-theistic, one presenting a major problem for creating any avatar. One of the major questions in comparative religion is: Does Buddhism have a deity? Some Buddhists claim that it does in the form of the first person to become a Buddha, but others claim that Siddhartha Gautama, the first, was only a royal human who found enlightenment. Although some questions arise, many followers of Buddhism, if not all, claim Buddhism is non-theistic, that is, lacking a deity.[49] There are a number of persons who have claimed they, like Siddhartha, achieved ultimate enlightenment, have become Bodhisattvas (highly enlightened) or even reincarnations of Siddhartha Gautama, the original *Buddha* or "enlightened one." Others have honored many persons as such or as reincarnations, thus as potential avatars. A much abbreviated listing of a few of the very many includes the following:

Section Two: Questions About Avatars—Gods Who Become Human

- Guan Yu, Chinese general in late Eastern Han Dynasty and Three Kingdoms period (died 220). [He was a serving army general who was said to have become the peace-loving manifestation of the Buddha.];

- Wu Zetian (624–705), a female Empress of China, who founded her own dynasty, the Second Zhou. [Fewer women than men have claimed or were claimed by others to be a Buddha.];

- Gung Ye (869–918), a Korean warlord and later King of Taebong, who ordered his servants to worship him.

- Nurhaci, known as Emperor Tai Zu (1559–1626), founder of the Qing Dynasty of China, who was believed by some to be a *Bodhisattva*, an enlightened person who, out of compassion, forsook nirvana to help others; Nurhaci was believed to be the Bodhisattva *Manjushri*;

- Mirza Ghulam Ahmed (1835–1908), who claimed to be the universal prophet for all religions including Buddhism; he founded a sect while preaching Islam as a universal faith for all;

- Peter Deunov (1864–1944, known as Master Beinsa Douno, who founded Esoteric Christianity and was considered a manifestation of *Maitreya*, the future Buddha. [The *Maitreya* was to be the final Buddha, coming at the end of time.];

- Ruth E. Norman, also known as Uriel (1900–1993), who said she had 55 past lives including: Buddha, King Arthur, Confucius, Socrates, and the King of Atlantis;

- Samael Aun Weor (1917–1977), a Columbian, author of over 60 books, who founded Universal Gnosticism, was said to be the *Maitreya*;

- Jim Jones (1931–1978) who founded the People's Temple cult, claimed to be an incarnation of the Buddha and also of Jesus. [In Guyana, he murdered over 900 members of his church by poisoning their communion.];

- Ariffin Mohammed (1943–2016), founder of the Sky Kingdom in Malaysia; he and his followers claimed he was an incarnation of Buddha, also the Islamic *Madhi*, a final times redeemer, as well as Muhammad, Jesus and Shiva;

- Claude Vorilhon, also known as Raël (1946–), who founded the Unidentified Flying Objects (UFO) religion; some claimed him the *Maitreya*;

Lu Sheng-yen (1945–), Taiwanese founder of the True Buddha School, claimed enlightenment in the 1980s and himself as the "Living Buddha Lian Sheng";

Ram Bahadur Bomjon (1990–), a Nepalese, who claimed that although Siddhartha Gautama, the original Buddha, reached *Sambuddha*, that is, self-enlightenment, he, Ram, had attained *Mahasambodhi*, a higher level than Siddhatha; he and his followers proclaim him as the *Maitreya*[50]

This is only a very partial list of Buddha claimants; there are many more. Buddhism is claimed by many adherents to be non-theistic, denying a creator deity. It does teach rebirth, with *nirvana* as the ultimate goal. A sage, when asked where Nirvana is, replied, "It is where light goes when you blow out the candle."

Not including those listed above, we must remember that it is almost only in Tibetan Buddhism that spiritual teachers become reincarnations of deceased masters but not deities; thus, they are not avatars.[51]

Given these examples, it is important to remember that an avatar must be a deity that has become incarnate. If Buddhism has no deity, there cannot be an avatar. Does this lack of possibility encourage the plethora of Buddha claimants?

The question arises: How can science help us understand these claimants who propose or whose followers propose they are reincarnations of the Buddha? The science of psychiatry is relatively new and surely would have much to say about this phenomenon. Some claimants could become a source of danger to their followers, for example, Jim Jones in Guyana. There are several psychological theories to account for this type of behavior.

On this question of many claimants, we truly need the help of science, and we cannot afford to allow a chasm between faith on the one hand and psychiatric science on the other to develop.

There are discoveries in psychology that would aid a new theology in understanding a person's belief in deity, and, more importantly, how a personal belief in God further aids a person's self-realization. A growing rapprochement between the church and psychology has led to classes in pastoral counseling in many seminaries, and these need to continue until clergy are more thoroughly trained. Those ordained shouldn't aspire to think themselves psychologists, but more training in psychology would aid nascent spiritual leaders.

Section Two: Questions About Avatars—Gods Who Become Human

Perhaps a more crucial question is whether humans have a mental disposition to believe in a deity, or actually possess the so-called god(s) gene, including a psychological need to pray, to congregate when performing rituals, and for some to take effective action for creating a better human society.

CHAPTER 21

War Leader Avatars in Islam?

IN ISLAM, THERE IS the concept of the *Madhi*, an end-of-times leader who will rule before the Day of Judgment, that is, the Day of Resurrection, and whose goal is the defeat of evil in the world. This concept has allowed some persons to be regarded as potential leaders possibly approaching avatar status in some followers's minds. There is no mention of the Madhi in the Koran, only in the later collections of the Ahadith, the Prophet Mohammad's teachings compiled by his followers after his death. In several traditions of Islam, the Madhi will arrive with, or slightly before, Issa (Jesus) to defeat the False Prophet or Antichrist.[52]

This concept of the Madhi has multiple persons claiming the title or having it imposed upon them. There are major differences of interpretations regarding the Mahdi between the Sunni and the Shiite branches of Islam, and there have been schisms in Islamic theology that have caused several separate sects to be established. For example, one sect is the Ahmadiyya, who believe Mirza Ghulam Ahmad (1835–1908) is both the Messiah and Mahdi, interpreting these as two terms designating the same person. The title *Messiah* means *appointed* by God while *Mahdi* means *guided* by God.[53]

Another Islamic sect, Mahdavia, was founded by Muhammad Jaunpuri (1443–1505), who claimed to be the Mahdi at the Kaaba in Mecca, Islam's most holy place, during the Pilgrimage (*Hijri*) and who was so regarded by his followers. They believed him to be the Imam Mahdi, the Caliph of Allah, and second in importance in Islam only to the Prophet Mohammad. Jaunpuri died in Afghanistan at the age of 63.[54]

Section Two: Questions About Avatars—Gods Who Become Human

Another claimant was Siyyid Ali Muhammad Shirází (1819–1850), who claimed to be the Madhi in 1844, adopting the name, Báb. He was the founder of Bábism. Executed in Tabriz the next year, he is buried in a tomb at the Baháʼí World Center in Haifa, Israel. The Baháʼí consider the Báb's announcement he was the Madhi as the beginning of the Baháʼí calendar.[55] Baháʼí includes several other religious leaders from history in its list of teachers.

Perhaps the most widely known claimant to be the Mahdi was Muhammad Ahmad, a Sudanese Sufi sheikh, who led a rebellion and created the state of Mahdliyah, carving it out of the Anglo-Egyptian Sudan in the latter half of the nineteenth century. He died several years after capturing the city of Khartoum, having had murdered many its inhabitants including its colonial governor, British General Charles George "Chinese" Gordon, so named for his service in the Chinese Opium Wars. Ahmad became known around the world for this conquest. Several years after his death, a British expedition marched down the Nile and recaptured Khartoum at the Battle of Omdurman. The initial slaughter in Khartoum created in the world press the mistaken concept of the Mahdi as a warrior conqueror who has his prisoners slain.[56] This mistaken concept, based almost solely on Khartoum, is patently false in Islamic theology.

In spite of these leader's followers's conjectures, mainstream Islam has always rejected any doctrine or concept of an incarnation of Allah in any form whatsoever, thus blocking any claim of avatar by anyone. Such a concept has an Arabic word describing it—*shirk*—meaning making something or someone equal to Allah, the practice of idolatry.[57] *Shirk* is a capital sin in Islam.

Some modern Islamic scholars also disagree about the concept of the Madhi. Abul Ala Maududi (1903–1979), an Islamic revivalist, thought the Madhi would become a reformer who unites the Ummah (all who believe in God) and thus converts the entire world to Islam. Maududi believed the Mahdi would never claim that title but only be recognized as such after his death.[58] Many Islamic scholars do not agree with Maududi's concepts of the Mahdi: Allama Tamanna Imadi (1888–1972), Allama Habbibur Rahman Kandhalvi (1994–1991), and Javed Ahmad Ghamidi (1951) are only a few.[59] Most Muslims believe the Mahdi comes at time's end.

Because of this doctrinal prohibition, there is no possibility of having an Islamic avatar, but a false Mahdi might come close to this belief in a twisted mind of an apocalyptic war leader. How such a concept could arise

War Leader Avatars in Islam?

in Islam is detailed in Yohanan Friedmann's book: *Prophesy Continuous: Aspects of Ahmadi Religious Thought and its Medieval Background.*

Yohanan Friedmann's thoughtful volume on Madhism is well researched. Timothy Furnish's *Holiest Wars: Islamic Mahdis, Jihad and Osama Bin Laden*, although interesting, was not well received by some Islamic theologians.

What is evident is that an avatar is impossible in Islam, such a claim being a major sin—*shirk*, attempting to be as great as Allah.

CHAPTER 22

Hinduism: Many Avatars

IT IS TO HINDUISM that we owe the word "avatar."[60] Hinduism is an amalgam of systems of ideas, beliefs, rituals, practices, and ways of living that represent perhaps the oldest religion except for primitive animism. The tradition can be traced, possibly, to figures engraved over several millennia ago in the Indus Valley, but is developed through the Vedic writings from the second millennium BCE. From these sources arose a multiplicity of sacred works. What characterizes Hinduism is a strong belief that any truth or concept of reality, either mental or material, is impossible to be adequately reported in a creed or statement of belief. Hindus insist that truth has to be sought in a plethora of sources and can never be dogmatically characterized. For these reasons, many followers of Hinduism regard it as not as a religion but as a way of life.[61]

Perhaps the most basic belief in Hinduism is *Brahman*, "an uncreated, eternal, infinite, transcendent, and all-embracing principle, which contains being and nonbeing and comprises the only reality. Brahman is the ultimate cause and from it emanates the universe and everything in it; it is the *Atman,* the self of all living things. Hindus differ on whether *Brahman*—"ultimate reality"—is best understood as a "personal God" or as the impersonal universal force; if the former, *Brahman* can be personalized by a large number of avatars—Vishnu, Shiva or Shakti, to name only three. Hinduism is ultimately the "search for a One that is the All," a search that has lasted over 3,000 years.[62]

Hinduism: Many Avatars

An *avatar* (from Sanskrit) is, "in Hinduism, the incarnation of a deity in human or animal form to counteract some particular evil in the world." Some examples would be:

> [T]he 10 appearances of *Vishnu*: *Matsya* (fish), *Kurma* (tortoise), *Varaha* (boar), *Narasimha* (half man, half lion), *Vamana* (dwarf), *Parashurama* (*Rama* with the axe), *Rama* (hero of the *Ramayana* epic), *Krishna* (the divine cowherd), *Buddha*, and *Kalkin* (the incarnation yet to come).[63]

The number of Vishnu's avatars is sometimes extended or their identities changed, according to local preferences. Thus, Krishna's half-brother, *Balarama*, is in some areas included as an avatar.[64]

Hindus believe in transmigration, the passage of souls from one form to another; this rebirth of the soul is determined by *karma*, that is, one's being good or evil. Rebirth, termed *samsara*, has no clear beginning or termination. The personal soul, *jiva*, faces eternal births and deaths unless released into the *Brahman* through collecting good karma. This release is termed *moksha*, when the individual soul realizes it is identical to the eternal Brahman, needing no identity whatsoever. There are several avenues by which to gain *moksha*; three are listed in influential order: *karma-marga*—"disinterested discharge of ritual and social obligations"; *jnana-marga*—"meditative concentration" to gain "a supra-intellectual insight into one's identity with *Brahman*"; and *bhakti-marga*—love for a personal God. It is this last avenue that seems to influence avatar realization.[65]

Why does Hinduism have so many avatars? We might tackle the question by seeing how the theological balance in Hinduism stands. On the one hand, we have an impersonal, eternal, creative, ultimate cause, foundation and goal of all existence, a universal source that is *Brahman*. There is nothing personal here, only force, fact, existence and goal, containing good and evil, everything and nothing. On the other hand, we have the avatars, anthropomorphic gods with personalities, their achievements and struggles mixing with human beings. In examining these two concepts of deity, one might see a human need to make deity approachable; thus, there occur human psychological *projections* influencing creation of the avatars. The vastness and almost unreachable nature of *Brahman* seems to require some means—perhaps *any* means—of personal approach, a way to symbolize it, an entity that persons can wrap their imaginations around in order to worship. On the eternal, unending, beyond-imaginable mental screen of the *Brahman*, a person can project various figures, just as we project numbers, "twoness" or "sevenness" to objects. These *projections*, a result of a natural, daily, human mental activity, probably needed for our understanding and for consciousness itself, become for Hindus the various avatars of not only Hinduism, but of all projected avatars in religious thought. C. G. Jung claims they are elements of archetypes and are created from the human collective unconscious just as other archetypes found in other religions.[66]

Besides projection, another psychological activity is the claiming of *identification* through *projection*. The child absorbs the parents's or the community's religious rites, beliefs, governance and duties, becoming personally identified with them along with the family. If the bond of family and/or community is ruptured or becomes obsolete, then a person might change belief systems by converting to a new religion that provides re-identification.[67]

From this perspective, we can see why even religions such as Islam or Judaism, which abhor and condemn the concept of avatars, have substitutes such as Madhism and persons claiming to be Messiahs. Crucial to the adoration of avatars are the psychological processes of *projection* and *identification*. Our identification with family, community, clan or ethnicity provides a great deal of what we believe in. It could be said that that identification can be political as well as religious. Civil religion was seen in Nazi Germany, in Communist acculturation, and in our own ritualistic political rallies and memorials. If a Marine is willing to die for what the US flag represents, isn't that a close archetypal similarity to someone dying for a religion as a martyr?

CHAPTER 23

Jainism: All Life is Holy

JAINISM IS ONE OF the major world religions that came from the Asian subcontinent, but differs from the other two, Buddhism and Hinduism. Each gives a different promise to its followers; Hinduism has the *Brahman* personified as an individual having an eternal self, an *atman*, while Buddhism promises that a person's soul is not necessarily permanent, capable of gaining *anatta*, that is, non-self, when reaching *nirvana*.

In Jainism there is a proposed *jiva*, a soul that is eternal but also changing. The *jiva* has living substance, but there is also an *ajiva*, divided into two beings that are material but nonsentient and those that are nonsentient and nonmaterial. *Jiva* is divided into mobile and immobile. What matters are how many of the five senses [touch, smell, hearing, taste, sight] a jiva has. The first group, material but nonsentient, has places in earth, water, fire and air; in this group, the vegetables possess only the sense of touch. The next group up the ladder has bodies and from two to five senses. A *jiva* takes on the elements of the body it occupies; at death, it takes on the shape/or physical body in which it was housed.[68]

In Jainism the *jiva* strives for the essentials—consciousness, bliss, and energy. Through time and the correct application of these essentials, the *jiva* may rid itself of *karma*, which for Jains is not, unlike Buddhism and Hinduism, a process but a substance. One must become free of karma and stop any further accretions of it through renunciation of passionate action.[69] Reality is constantly arising, changing, and decaying, and only by reaching the state of omniscience can one be free of karma. This theological

Section Two: Questions About Avatars—Gods Who Become Human

concept differs from the Hindu concept, where reality is permanent, and from Buddhist where it is impermanent.[70]

In Jainism, knowledge short of omniscience is flawed, and the best practice to gain insight is yoga, which is practiced especially by the monks. Jainism had several splits into sects, but their most crucial difference is between those that are the Digambara (sky clad) and the Svetembara (white clad). Both have their own theological positions on the nature of attachment as well as on violence. Both have their own differing scriptures.[71]

There are monks and nuns in Jainism as well as laity. Monks of the Digambara usually are naked (sky clad), but nuns are allowed to wear white. Women must be reborn into a man's body to further advance to omniscience. Monks and nuns of the Svetembara wear white (cloud clad). Monks can be seen sweeping the path as they walk so as not to harm any living creatures.[72]

For the followers of Jainism time and the universe are eternal and uncreated. Time is understood as a gigantic wheel with twelve spokes or ages, six of which ascend and six descend. The wheel keeps turning, repeating each age, time after time. Jain doctrine precludes liberation from the wheel in the present because the current age is viewed as corrupt and descending. Only by living a life of nonviolence and progressing in discipline and service may one slowly advance to another rebirth nearer to *moksha*, eternal liberation from rebirths.[73]

Jainism stands midway between Buddhism, which seeks enlightenment to achieve *nirvana*, human identity joining with pure consciousness and dissolving, and Hinduism, which seeks final personal attachment to the *Brahman* as an individual soul through right living and ritual. In the same way, a Hindu approaches the vastness of *Brahman*, which is both being and non-being, and the Buddhist approaches impermanence, that is, non-being. The Jains approach the *Living* part of an eternal universe. They treasure each and every life, and although they eat vegetables—necessary to sustain life—the gift of life to every creature and anything else alive is treasured. The measure to which Jains go to protect and respect life provides the possibility that their deity is ultimately seen in the fact of *Living*, no matter in what form that living might be present.[74]

From this theological perspective, considering that many Jains believe that the religion had no historical founder, there seems little chance for Jainism to provide an avatar; however, there were the 24 Tirthankaras, the last of whom, Vardhamana, the Mahavira or Great Hero, a contemporary of

Guatama the Buddha, is important because of his story. The word Tirthankara means "ford maker" and "they build passages to allow their followers to cross from suffering and pain to happiness." Mahavira's life story constitutes an important part of Jainism's scripture. Thus there is, in Jainism, the possibility of a man becoming a *kevalin*, a possessor of omniscience, in time becoming a Tirthankara; however, not all *kevalins* are Tirthankaras, for becoming one "requires the development of a particular type of karmic destiny." They are still just humans and not deities, so even if they come close, they do not qualify as avatars.[75]

Biology and botany and their related sciences might provide the elements for understanding just what it means *to be alive*. There are still questions about whether viruses are alive. Besides physicists and astronomers, psychologists, historians and the other scientists previously mentioned, it seems necessary for the human race to find *exactly what life is* and how it comes about.

Buddhism asks us how we might approach nothingness. Hinduism asks us how we might approach eternal being, "is-ness," ontology itself. Jainism asks us what it means for something to be alive. Is *life* itself a gift of divinity or a result of natural forces in the universe or both? Science can help us in seeking an answer.

CHAPTER 24

Shinto: Ritual, Kami, Nature

SHINTO IS ARGUABLY MORE a daily practice, a philosophical way of living, than a religion *per se*. It does pay tribute, which some might see as worship, to the *kami*, who are termed *gods* but are spirits concerned with human beings. The *kami*, if honored correctly, are thought to help persons succeed in gaining a good life and health. In this way Shinto is a view of the ways of the world and of nature, and encourages the practice of necessary rituals. Shinto was once the official but is now an unofficial national religion of Japan, with family shrines in homes and larger shrines scattered around the nation. These draw some people daily and more on holidays. The major element in Shinto is ritual and not necessarily devout belief.[76]

There appear to be no avatars in Shinto, although the Japanese emperors were once regarded as holy and descendants of the *kami*. A Japanese explanation of the word *kami* was given by Motoori Norinaga, described as "one of the most distinguished Japanese scholars of religion and enthusiasts for Shinto revival":

> I do not yet understand the meaning of the word 'kami.' In the most general sense, it refers to all divine beings of heaven and earth that appear in the classics. More particularly, the kami are the spirits that abide in and are worshipped at shrines.[77]

Another explanation reports that "*Kami* as a property is the sacred or mystical element in almost everything. It is in everything and found everywhere, and is what makes an object itself rather more than something else."[78]

Shinto: Ritual, Kami, Nature

Amaterasu-Omikami, the greatest of the *kami* and known as the Sun Goddess, is regarded as the ancestor of the Imperial family; thus, Japanese Emperors were regarded as sacred and worshipped. They would not be defined as avatars because *kami* are not transcendent or omnipotent, their non–deistic status reflected in their actions, human foibles and follies.[79] On January 1, 1946, the Emperor Hirohito proclaimed that the emperor of Japan was not to be considered divine.[80]

In Shinto, human beings are born free from sin. They share part of the divine soul, but *tsumi*, pollution, can affect persons who are mature (not children) and *tsumi* includes impurity, physical or spiritual, and results in bad manners and moral slights. Shinto provides cleansing and purifying rituals; cleanliness is regarded as a daily, obligatory ritual. Death or anything dead are particularly polluting.[81] Since the emperors were not truly gods but supposed descendants of a *kami*, they were defined spirit. Shinto does not have, by definition, any avatars.

Shinto places a high regard on good manners, respect for others, the rightful fulfilling of obligations. Minus the *kami*, it resembles an ethic more than a religion.

CHAPTER 25

Confucianism: Being Respectful

CONFUCIANISM IS AN ANCIENT practice in China, and it is difficult to examine it as a religion instead of as a philosophical stance and a deity-lacking ethics with attached ritual practices. It is based on the thought of the Chinese teacher, K'ung Fu-tzu, that is, Kong the Master (BCE 551–479), known in the West as Confucius. This "ethicslogy's" rituals and practices are derived from *The Analects*, a collection of writings by the master teacher and his contemporaries and students. These ideas are still the template "of learning, the source of values, and the social code of the Chinese," although they have been somewhat displaced by Maoist Communism.[82]

Confucianism is not an organized religion; its namesake did not set out to make it so. Kong Fu-tzu "considered himself a transmitter who consciously tried to reanimate the old order to attain the new," primarily by outlining a "ritualized life" that reinforced "reverence for ancestors, human-centered religious practices, and mourning ceremonies." A natural extension of these ideas is centered in what is called ancestor worship, a ritual for ceremonial worship of forebearers.[83] The *Analects* (*Lanyu*) can be compared to the Platonic dialogues in their origin, being based on "succeeding generations of Confucius's disciples." Some critics may look on *The Analects* as "a collection of unrelated reflections randomly put together." However, these are not just moral snippets, for if you view them as "communal memory," they become a manual for understanding Confucius's concepts of "self-knowledge" and, in turn, they lead to a person's own self-understanding. Central to Confucius's thought was the idea of continuous

Confucianism: Being Respectful

education of the person throughout life, the "ceaseless process of self-realization." Two major goals were "culture (*wen*)" and "learning (*xue*)."[84]

Followers of Kong Fu-tsu (an alternative spelling) believe that everyone is at heart good, and that you should respect and obey your elders, that your ancestors should be venerated not as deities but as worthy persons, that education is every human's task, and that Yin and Yang, opposing forces in the universe, will balance out "everything." Beliefs to be emulated are:

> *Ren*: ideal treatment of others; *Li*: ritual, propriety, etiquette; *Hsiao*, love within the family, love of children by parents and children for parents; *Yi*: righteousness; *Xin*: honesty, trustworthiness; *Jen* benevolence, humaneness towards others. The highest Confucian virtue, *Chung*: loyalty to the state.[85]

There is no afterlife in Confucianism, and other than ancestor "worship" there seems to be a hiatus of daily ritual except for polite and respectful interaction between people and the constant search for knowledge. The concern is to live life harmoniously and to fit comfortably into your society. There is "one great deity and the lord of heaven which is worshipped" through seasonal sacrifices offered by state practitioners, most formally by the emperor;[86] however, these ceremonies have disappeared in today's Maoism, sometimes replaced by a veneration of Mao. When well-trained Communist Chinese refer to someone who has died, they often say: "He has gone to Mao."[87]

Confucianism has no avatars, not even its namesake.

CHAPTER 26

Taoism: Sensitivity to All

TAOISM (PRONOUNCED "DAOISM," WHICH sounds closer to the Chinese pronunciation) is a belief system that seems to be a religion still instructive for Chinese. It arose from Lao Tzu's (c. 500 BCE) *Tao-Te-Ching* (*The Tao*), that is, *The Way*. The Tao is not a personal deity; rather it is the "ultimate creative principle of the universe." In the Tao, all matter and actions are interconnected either as a unity or its opposites—*Yin* and *Yang*, "action and inaction, light and dark, hot and cold." Not being a deity, the Tao is not worshipped, but there are very many projected personalities venerated in Taoist temples. These figures represented by statues are just "a part of the universe and depend, like everything, on the Tao."[88] No true avatars exist in Taoism, only projected archetypes.

A visit to Tai Shan (Tranquil Mountain), the foremost of Taoism's five sacred peaks,[89] provides insight into Taoism's effect on visitors. In its temple courtyard, as I was listening to the birds' soft calls, alone from the crowd lining up for the funicular, I felt a growing sense of calm. Relaxing there in the evening as the sun set and twilight gleamed, my senses appreciated a mood of tranquility, enhanced by a softening feeling of peace and calm and the holy as the breeze wafted down from the heights, gently cooling, slowly moving the tree branches. Doves were cooing in the cool evening air, all of nature feeling peaceful at Tai Shan.

The next morning, while treading up the steep stairs near the top, I saw a Taoist pilgrim, an elderly man, who knelt at each step, bowed, and recited prayers, doing so at each step up the 1,545-meter mountain.[90] He was on the third and last day of his climb up the mountain's steep stone stairway.

We silently passed him, noticing the multitude of old carved stone stele memorials bearing comments from or about Chinese emperors, generals and dignitaries. The first emperor of China, Qin Shi-huangdi, who had started building the Great Wall, scaled Tai Shan in the third century BCE. To do so became almost a requirement for each emperor or senior politician since then.[91]

Later, at the top, after stops to appreciate the views, I paused to watch that same Taoist pilgrim finishing his three-day tiring climb. It was emotionally moving seeing him reach the final step, pray, stand up, then walk very stiffly from tired knees toward the summit's temples while seeing the morning sun, a symbol of rebirth and renewal. An elderly, simple pilgrim had reached his destination that day observing "The Way."

It is said that Kong Fu-tzu (Confucius) climbed the stairs at Tai Shan. Many still do to this day, grandparents, adults, children, those on a spiritual quest and others only on vacation. Scaling Tai Shan or one of the other mountains sacred to Taoism was built into Chinese life millennia ago. The palatial temple at its base is dedicated to China's San Shan, another name for Tai Shan, and it has been said it is the "largest mountain-spirit shrine in the world, ranking with only the emperor's palace in Beijing and the Confucius Family Shrine in Qufu as a traditional Chinese complex." Tai Shan is not just a holy place similar to Mt. Olympus or Mt. Sinai; it was once regarded as a deity itself, venerated by the Chinese for centuries as their most sacred peak, regarded by the emperors as an actual son of the Emperor of Heaven, giving them heaven's mandate to rule. When the emperor came, the entire retinue would be so large that it would stretch from the bottom to the summit, over 7,000 steps, a distance of six miles up a steep stairway.[92] Mao Ze-dong climbed Tai Shan to follow in the steep steps of China's emperors.[93] The final section, as you can see, does not have a funicular.

Tai Shan is still revered by many Taoist. Although thus revered, it is not regarded as a representative of any specific deity and, therefore, not an avatar. It is regarded as a divine mountain, a sacred place, but not a god.

Section Two: Questions About Avatars—Gods Who Become Human

Final Steps to the summit of Tai Shan

With mountains and emperors as holy spirits but now not deities, one would not expect to find any human avatars present in Taoism; not surprisingly, there are none. Taoism's energy is psychological, spiritual, and ultimately personal. Its impact is still embedded in Chinese life, along with

Confucianism, but unlike the latter, does not have ancestor "worship." Lao Tzu is not an avatar, only a teacher of knowledge about life and how to live.

Taoism's import is ultimately mindful and spiritual, an appreciation of "what is," helpful for gaining emotional balance. It seems to inculcate in a person a means to grasp an assured gentility in living and interaction with all other things. Its deepest meaning seems to be the idea of accepting what life has to offer and abiding with and appreciating its outcomes.

There is a Chinese legend I learned from a retired Chinese scholar while teaching in Nanjing. Long ago a scholar searched for the ideal location to build his family's new home. He found it high on a mountain, but there was another rugged mountain that blocked the view to a very beautiful valley. The scholar had several sons and one morning as he sat looking at the mountain blocking his view of the wondrous valley, he meditated. He announced to the Eight Chinese Immortals—who by legend are supposed to oversee the world—that he would start the next day with his sons to level the high cliffs blocking his desired view. The scholar said he realized that it might take multiple generations, but with hard work by his descendants they would take down the mountain so the beautiful valley would be visible from their ancestral home. The next day, on arising, the scholar noticed the mountain no longer blocked his view of the delightful valley. When he asked the Eight Immortals how that was possible, they replied that his and his descendents's strong persistence so moved them that they had lowered the blocking mountain.

These eight immortals are not avatars; they are personifications of human traits and projections of basic goodness; they are understood as reflections of abilities associated with the tasks of living.[94]

That fable of the wise scholar and his sons has always stood for me as the core of Taoism—calm persistence with optimistic acceptance. Taoism seems to provide a willingness to contemplate our own multigenerational perspectives, trusting in hard work and the aid of heaven. It can be characterized by a phrase: "Always strive to progress with the flow of nature appreciating the joy of living."

CHAPTER 27

Sikhism: Serving, Living, Duty

SIKHISM HAS A SINGLE deity. Sikhs regard religious rites as "superstitions [which] have no value." To their deity, who lacks form or gender, every person has access and is equal. Creating "a good life as part of a community, . . . honesty and caring for others," and meditating are the way to living fully and completely. Locked in "a cycle of birth, life, and rebirth," a Sikh wants "to share . . . beliefs with followers of other . . . religious traditions." Karma can limit the quality of life because of the way a person lived in a former life, and to escape this fate a Sikh must "achieve a total knowledge of and union with God. Truth is one of the highest of all virtues, but higher still is truthful living."[95]

Founded in India by Guru Nanak in the fifteenth century, Sikhism regards holiness as living benevolently and understanding everyday problems. In Sikhism, God is beyond proper understanding; however, it is possible for Sikhs to experience God through acts of "love, worship, and contemplation," thereby finding the divine "in themselves and in the world around them." The Sikh's holy place is the Golden Temple, Amritsa, India. For them, God is inside of everyone. "no matter how wicked."

A good Sikh serves God by also serving (*seva*) other people every day.[96] There are three Sikh requirements for action: "*Nam Japna*, keeping God in mind at all times"; "*Kirt Karna*, earning an honest living," which includes not only avoiding criminal activity but also no "gambling, begging, or working in the alcohol or tobacco industries"; *Vand Chhakna*, "giving to charity and caring for others."[97]

Sikhism: Serving, Living, Duty

Noticeable to others are the symbols of the "Khalisa initiation," signs that mark many Sikh believers—the Five Ks; these are *Kesk*, uncut hair; *Kara*, a steel bracelet; *Kanga*, a wooden comb; *Kaccha*, cotton underwear; and *Kirpan*, a steel sword. These requirements date from the "creation of the *Khalsa Panth* by Guru Gobind Singh in 1699."[98] Guru Gobind Singh introduced these initiation requirements so the "symbols would identify members of the Khalisa, because all members who wear these are more strongly bound to each other, and because each symbol has a particular significance for those who have been initiated." The Khalsa serves as a military group of men and women dedicated to defend Sikhism.[99]

The martial aspect of the religion began under Guru Arjan, the fifth Guru, who made Amritsar the Sikh capital and "compiled the first authorized Sikh scripture, the *Adi Granth*." At this time, the religion, so distinctive from Hinduism and Islam, came under attack, and Guru Arjan was executed in 1606. The sixth, Guru Hargobind, further "militarized" the Sikhs, for they had to fight "battles to preserve the faith" and the community. With the reign of the Moghal Emperor, Aurangzeb, there was renewed "force to make his subjects accept Islam," and "Aurangzeb had the ninth Guru, Tegh Bahadar," executed in 1675. It was the tenth, Guru Gobind Singh, who recreated the Sikhs into a standing militarized force through the Khalsa in 1699. The Sikhs continued their militarization with Banda Singh Bahadar; however, he was captured and executed in 1716. Later, the Sikhs again revolted and over the next 50 years took over more and more territory. In 1799, Ranjit Singh captured Lahore, and in 1801 established the Punjab as an independent state, with himself as maharaja. Relations then eased with other religions until the conquest by the British, who in "1845 began defeating the Sikh army and took over the Punjab." The Sikhs revolted again in 1849, along with many other rebelling groups across India, but they were defeated.[100]

After this defeat, recognizing the quality of Sikh military training, the British put them into the celebrated British Indian Army Sikh regiments.[101]

"Good relations between Sikhs and the British came to an end in 1919 with the Amritsar massacre," where British troops fired on over 10,000 worshippers at the Sikh's most revered and important religious celebration at the Golden Temple, killing over 400 and wounding over 1,000. Another massacre was repeated after the independence of India (August 15, 1947). The Sikhs had bargained then for an independent state in the Punjab, but their request was denied.[102] A Sikh religious leader in 1983 inflamed crowds

Section Two: Questions About Avatars—Gods Who Become Human

over this issue and several others, and after warnings from Delhi, retreated with his followers to the Golden Temple. In June 1984, Indira Gandhi, Prime Minister of India, ordered an attack on the Golden Temple which killed many inside and severely damaged buildings. This "abomination" of their most sacred place infuriated the Sikhs.[103]

Many saw Indira Gandhi as a persecutor of their religion, and in October 1984, two of Gandhi's Sikh bodyguards assassinated her. "Four days of anti-Sikh rioting followed," with the official government report stating that more that 2,700 people, mostly Sikhs, were killed, while newspapers and human rights groups put the death toll between 10,000 and 17,000.[104]

Although the ten Gurus were instrumental in founding and furthering the Sikh faith, after the death of the last Guru, the Sikh scriptures replaced them. One of the major Sikh rituals observed at the Golden Temple in Amritsar is when the scriptures are paraded around the temple. Sikhs there then bow and reverently respect their scriptures as the source of their faith and life.[105] Both of the attacks on the Golden Temple by the British in 1919 and by the Indian Army occurred during this sacred festival at Amritsar.

With this history of combat and civic conflict with military leaders and martyrs for the cause, there were multiple opportunities for a Sikh avatar to arise; however, none appeared. Could the strict requirements of the Khalisas bar such a possibility or is there another reason why no Sikh avatar could appear?

The Gurus were only enlightened teachers, not avatars. Sikhism, though having a history that might produce an avatar, did not have one appear.

CHAPTER 28

Bahá'í: Synoptic Goals—Seeking Peace

THE BAHÁ'Í FAITH STARTED in Iran with what was regarded as two divine messengers: the first was the Báb (1819–1850) and the second was Mirza 'Ali Nuri, known as Bahá'u'lláh (1817–1892).[106] It is the writings of the latter that constitute most of Bahá'í scriptures. The Báb served as a bearer of an important message; his mission was to prepare the way for a coming second messenger who would bring "an age of peace and justice" to the world. That messenger was Bahá'u'lláh (the "Glory of God"), "the Promised One foretold by the Báb and all of the Divine Messengers of the past." These Messengers were believed to be "Manifestations of God—Abraham, Krishna, Zoroaster, Moses, Buddha, Jesus Christ, Muhammad."[107]

Bahá'ís believe that there is one all-powerful deity who creates and progressively reveals divinity through the major religions of the world, the revelations coming from many of the founders of multiple religions. They have no clergy, and each community governs itself.

They do not hold or follow what they would regard as superstitions but insist on the unhindered search for scientific and religious truth. Thus, the Bahá'ís include scientific discoveries in their theology. The highest goals for humans to meet are the highest moral standards. They work for world peace, and they labor to create a united global commonwealth, acknowledging the unity of all religions and unity of all mankind without regard for gender or race.[108]

'Abdu'l-Bahá, the oldest son of Bahá'u'lláh, became the leader of the faith after being named so in his father's will. 'Abdu'l-Bahá strived to become an ambassador of peace and a good exemplar of the new faith. His

Section Two: Questions About Avatars—Gods Who Become Human

grandson, Shoghi Effendi, the next leader, for 36 years carefully nurtured the development and understanding of the faith and Bahá'í unity, so it "increasingly grew to reflect the diversity of the entire human race."[109] Bahá'í today is directed by the Universal House of Justice in Haifa, Israel, which instructs Bahá'ís "to exert a positive influence on the welfare of humankind, promote education, peace and global prosperity, and safeguard human honor and religion." Under the guidance of the Universal House of Justice, Bahá'ís continue to practice "acts of devotion, such as prayer, meditation, fasting, pilgrimage, and service to others."[110]

As an amalgam of religious beliefs and with its aim of world peace, Bahá'í does draw an increasing number of adherents around the world. In the Bahá'í faith there is no avatar, no one who could be an incarnation of God.

Chapter 29

Judaism: Being Chosen Has a Price

JUDAISM'S BELIEF IS THAT this world has a purpose and that a non-physical, single God created it. Jews also believe that each person has a soul, existing after death, and that this soul is held responsible for a person's action in this life. Any person, Jewish or not, by living by God's laws gains equal reward after death.[111]

Moses Maimonides, a major Jewish theologian and medical pioneer, listed the essential beliefs of Judaism often memorized by children in *schul*:

1. God exists and created all that has being; therefore, the world is not without purpose or riddled with chaos.

2. God is single, alone, and unique, a concept given to the world by Abraham, the father of at least two faiths, Judaism and Islam; Abraham's descendants regard the deity as the center and creator of all reality.

3. God is not physical nor should any other thing or person ever be worshipped; there are no god-kings, no demigods, and no angels who revolt from God.

4. God is eternal and has always been so, and God's ways are also eternal, not capricious, forgetful or fickle, so maintaining a valid relationship with God is the sole activity that creates eternal benefits.

5. Prayer is only spoken to God, to nothing else.

6. The words of the prophets are true, for what was declared by the prophets in the *Tanakh* [Hebrew scriptures] have been coming true throughout history.

Section Two: Questions About Avatars—Gods Who Become Human

7. Moses, who led the Hebrews out of Egyptian slavery, prophesied what was true and he is the greatest prophet.
8. The *Torah* [the first five books of the *Tanakh*] was given to Moses by God, and it is the center of Jewish life; Jews must keep *Mitzvot* (God's commands), for the Torah is the single most precious thing; it is the foundation of the religion.
9. The Torah is unique; there will be no other; all that is new must be measured against the laws of the Torah, both written and oral [the oral Torah was that also given to Moses on Sinai].
10. God, whose name is holy, is aware of the actions and even the thoughts of all people.
11. God rewards the good and punishes the evil and is always righteous, even forgiving, to those who truly repent.
12. The Messiah will come and the dead will be resurrected.[112]

For Jews the Torah is a living law since the written Torah is being understood through the oral Torah and vice versa. For Jews God is a unity; there are no other divinities, a belief which immediately rules out avatars. A land in the Middle East (known today as *Eretz Yisrael*) stands as a bond between God and the Hebrews, going back to the Torah's promise to Abraham (Genesis 10:18–29; Ezekiel 20:42).[113]

> Jews hold the Sabbath, the seventh day of the week (Saturday) as holy, and worship then as well as on special holidays including Passover, the New Year and the Day of Atonement. All adults are responsible through their own free will, and on Yom Kipper (the Day of Atonement) can repent and receive absolution by God; however, absolution can be given any time when repentance is genuine.[114]

The only prophet translated to heaven was Elijah (2 Kings 2:1–11). He has always been seen in Judaism as an auspicious provider for the poor or oppressed, for God supplied food for him in the wilderness (1 Kings 17:1–7). In some Jewish congregations, one might see a chair hanging on a wall; it is reserved for Elijah. At a Passover Seder, there is an empty chair at the table provided for Elijah, and during the ceremony, a child is sent to the door to see if Elijah might have arrived to join in the Seder.

This interest in a visit by the prophet Elijah is not regarded as a reverence for an avatar, even though Elijah was translated to heaven. Elijah is only a prophet, although a major one. He is one of many who remind Jews

Judaism: Being Chosen Has a Price

of how anyone can live a sanctified life following instructions in the Torah. Neither Elijah nor anyone else could be an avatar; such would be an impossibility in Jewish theology.

This reality has not kept many people from claiming to be the Messiah; unfortunately, history is filled with persons announcing themselves to have gained this goal or having others so proclaim. There are numerous Jewish claimants for the title of Messiah; a few selected names of those are:

Simon bar Kokhba (died c. 135);

Moses of Crete (fifth century);

Ishak ben Ya'kub Abu 'Isa al-Isfahani (684–705);

David Alroy (c. 1160);

Moses Botarel (c. 1413);

Asher Lämmlein (c. 1502);

David Reubeni (1490–541?);

Solomon Molcho (1500–1532);

Sabbatai Zevi (1626–1676);

Jacob Querido (?—1690);

Miguel Cardoso (1630–1706);

Löbele Prossnitz (?—1750);

Jacob Joseph Frank (1726–1791);

Yosef Yitzchak Schneersohn (r.1880–1950); Lubovitch rebbe;

Menachem Mendel Schneersohn (1902–1994), Yosef Yatzchak's son-in-law.[115]

The effects of a false claimant can be seen in Isaac Bashevis Singer's novel, *Satan in Goray*, where a village suffers from its followers of Sabbatai Zevi, a historical false Messiah (see above list).[116] The novel allows readers to see the massive amount of *"tsuris"* created by such claims (*tsuris* in Yiddish means troubles or aggravations). Singer's insights provide a clear example of what happens when a false messiah comes and overturns society and the religion. Judaism seems rightfully not to trust avatars including false Messiahs. This fact seems to mark a major difference between Judaism and Christianity.

CHAPTER 30

Christianity I: Avatar's Time/Place

CHRISTIANITY, AS ITS NAME demands, is a religion based specifically on an avatar. The belief is that *Yeshua ben Yosef* [Jesus' name in Hebrew], a carpenter from Nazareth, was the Son of God, born miraculously via virgin birth in Judea. He worked possibly for three years as an itinerant teacher [rabbi] and was crucified by the Romans. The foundation of the faith is that he was resurrected from the dead on the Sunday following his execution on Friday in Jerusalem. The appellation, *Christ*, in Greek *Christos* or in Hebrew *Meshiah* (Messiah), means "the anointed." It designates that early Christians believed Yeshua was the *anointed* descendant of King David and, for most of them, the Son of God.[117]

Having an avatar as an incarnated God presents some difficult problems theologically. These need to be raised here so you might see how some Christian theologians seek to answer them. When you have an avatar, you have distinctive characteristics: time, place, gender, proof of divinity, proof of truthful reportage of the events, and how an incarnated body is perceived. Let's study some of these, one at a time.

TIME: It is believed that Yeshua or to use his Hellenized name, Jesus, was born during the reign of Herod the Great, King of Judea (Luke 1:5), a Roman vassal state on the Eastern shore of the Mediterranean. Yeshua did not live on Earth long enough to see the complete military subjugation of Judea by the Roman legions. Since the supposed date of his birth marks how Western Civilization enumerates the Current Era (CE), it is extremely difficult to date his life without referring to its beginning. Most scholars now believe that it was several years earlier than once supposed because of some clues in scriptures.

Luke 2:1–3, for example, mentions that the first census of Governor Quirinius, ordered by Caesar Augustus, was what made Joseph and Mary journey to Bethlehem where Yeshua was born. This census for taxation was ordered by Caesar Augustus in 4 BCE. There is thus a good chance that Yeshua was born in 4 to 3 BCE; scholars believe it was in Spring or early Autumn, approximately six months after John the Baptist was born (Luke 1:36–80; 2:7). Church councils established the Christmas date of December 25 several centuries later; thus, the celebrated time of Yeshua's birth is questionable.

PLACE: It is believed that Yeshua was born in the town of Bethlehem (Luke 2:4–7; Matthew 2:1), known as the City of David, for King David was born there. Yeshua's ministry, considered by scholars to have lasted about three years, was as an itinerant rabbi teaching around the Sea of Galilee with a group of disciples.

Although Judea was occupied by Roman legionnaires, King Herod had his own royal troops and the Temple in Jerusalem had its armed guards. Judaism was the official religion of the small nation centered on the rebuilt Temple in Jerusalem on Mount Zion; however, there were also the Samaritans, whose temple was in the north on Mount Gerizim.[118]

The Samaritans are a group related to the Jews. They believed they were the ones who did not suffer the Babylonian captivity after the conquest of Jerusalem and today are descendants of the once northern Kingdom of Samaria, separate from Judea. At Herod's death, his kingdom was divided into thirds for his three sons with the elder, Archelaus, gaining Judea and Samaria; in 6 CE, Archelaus was deposed and replaced by a Roman governor.[119]

Growing up in Nazareth probably presented some problems for young Yeshua. He had to go to the synagogue to be taught, which must have provided him a successful education, for it is mentioned in Luke 2:41–52, when, during a family Passover trip to Jerusalem, Yeshua disappeared for three days, causing major concern for his parents until they returned and found him in the Temple, sitting among the scholars, answering questions and amazing the priests and rabbis with his insights. Evidently, they did not regard him as a typical young man, which had to cause Yeshua and his family some major concern when word about what happened at the temple got back to Nazareth.

Section Two: Questions About Avatars—Gods Who Become Human

It is very difficult to be an avatar when everyone in town knows who you are and has seen you growing up day after day. Yeshua probably worked with Joseph in his carpenter's shop. Ironically, one of the major contracts a carpenter might receive from the occupying Roman legions was for crosses for executions. Imagine the irony of Yeshua and Joseph fulfilling an order for crosses from the *adiutor* (Roman legion supply assistant) of the local legion's occupying cohort.

According to Luke 3:23, Yeshua began his ministry when he was about 30 years old. How Yeshua's neighbors and fellow citizens reacted to this beginning of his teaching can be seen in Luke 4:16–30. Having successfully taught in synagogues around the Sea of Galilee, Yeshua returned to Nazareth and on the Sabbath went to his local synagogue where he had earlier customarily worshiped. When he was asked to read from the *Tanakh*, he quoted Isaiah 61:1–2 and 58:6. Yeshua seemed to anticipate the congregation's reaction, for he is reported to have said: "Truly, I say to you, no prophet is acceptable in his own country." (Luke 4:24). After Yeshua made several comments on the text, some worshippers became angry, and they took him out of the town to a high hill where they could throw him off, but Yeshua walked through the mob and went away. It would have been rather difficult for Joseph and Mary to continue to live in Nazareth after that incident. It also might have been dangerous for Yeshua to stay. What happened after this in Nazareth we don't know, nor do we know how Joseph and Mary fared there from then on.

This mob activity at the synagogue illustrates the many problems of humans who grow up in a normal way and claim avatar status, that is, being divine as the Messiah. The neighborhood probably would not have liked his declaration very much. According to Luke 4:16–30, some people in Nazareth became very angry. Growing up in Nazareth might have produced a very difficult childhood for Yeshua; people often have long memories. One can imagine reactions when neighbors learn that the boy whom they saw grow up became a teacher who claims to be the Messiah. One can easily imagine the chatter of the community:

"Hey, I know him. They lived around the corner."
"Sure, we went to *schul* together."
"Who does he think he is, now claiming he's Messiah?"
"We're just as good as he is, aren't we?"

One can understand how the local people could become very angry. It is important that not all Jews or other people reacted as did those worshippers at the synagogue in Nazareth. If you believe that an avatar, a "son of the deity," has provided your answers to life's crucial questions and see that that avatar's neighbors have not accepted him, even though these people claim a covenantal relationship to God, then wouldn't it be rather easy to disparage people who don't accept the avatar, that is, the Jews. Apparently, that was not the case during Yeshua's ministry, for it is recorded in the gospels that he preached to large crowds. They listened and eventually with others later started the church. Why then are the avatar's people who did not follow him not accepted? Yeshua was a Jew. Were they not Yeshua's first followers? God chose the Jews for the people of the Incarnation. Do they deserve antipathy from anyone for being God's choice?

CHAPTER 31

Christianity II: Avatar's Gender

GENDER: ACCORDING TO LUKE 2:21, Jesus was circumcised and named Yeshua (in Hebrew יֵשׁוּעַ) or *Iësous* (in Greek), the latter having in English a pronunciation similar to Jesus. These names are derived from the Hebrew phrase "The Lord is Salvation."[120] The fact that Yeshua was circumcised, as were all Jewish male children, proves his gender as male, since Hebrews and later the Jews never practiced female circumcision. Circumcision was done as a part of the ritual called *brit milah* in Hebrew or a *bris* in Yiddish.

An avatar having a gender, either male or female, provides a special status since the deity chose that gender for being on Earth. It raises immediate problems for the gender *not* chosen. Granted that the masculine was the dominant gender in Judea at the time of Yeshua and for many centuries, that selection still rings down the centuries, causing multiple problems.

The early church, recognizing gender equality in the new born religion, recognized this potential problem, since it allowed women to have major positions and functions.[121] However, over the ensuing centuries, with masculine leadership nearly always holding a monopoly, the role of female leadership outside of sainthood became almost nonexistent. Abbess Hildegard of Bingen was one of the few medieval women theological leaders. Hildegard wasn't a church hierarch, only an abbess. For centuries women had secondary powers and roles. The church is now, after almost two millennia, recognizing the possible potential role of leadership for women once again.

It took centuries for the Catholic Church to recognize the crucial theological role of the feminine. On December 8, 1854, Pope Pius IX published the Apostolic Constitution *Ineffabilis Deus*, which declared that the Virgin Mary "... was preserved free from all stain of original sin ..." in her conception in the womb of her mother, St. Anne.[122] This raises an interesting question: Was the Blessed Virgin Mary—known today among other titles as Queen of Angels—an avatar, since she was conceived immaculately? The answer by theologians would probably be negative since she is *not* recognized as part of the Trinity, which is made of Father, Son and Holy Spirit; however, it does elevate the BVM (Blessed Virgin Mary) to an *almost* divine status, as seen by her various titles and the frequent recitation of the rosary.

It is unfortunate that it took centuries for recognition of the importance of feminine contributions to Christian living, and some female Roman Catholics still await their full recognition. The monopoly of the masculine in the priesthood has proven to be a marked hardship for the Catholic Church, for there are now coming to light many instances of abuse by priests of people, both boys and girls, both young and old. This problem has toppled administrative church leaders: cardinals, bishops, priests, ministers, denominational leaders.

As the research on women's roles in the early church grows, it allows us to wonder whether the monopoly of masculinity over the centuries in the priesthood may be partially responsible for the instances of abuse we are now reading about. One must admit that masculinity does not have a monopoly on abuse. An example was the physical and psychological horror of women in the Magdalene Laundries in Ireland, only one example of others where nuns were responsible for female abuse.[123] Historical examples amply depict that abuse of children and women and even men is far from exclusively a Roman Catholic problem. It is too widespread in many denominations and faiths, mostly enacted psychologically but unfortunately not always.

It is rather difficult to observe these crises arising around the world without wondering whether it would *not* be happening if women were allowed to some roles of the priesthood or even if priests were allowed to marry. I will never forget my surprise in Veliko Turnovo, Bulgaria, when I saw a priest pushing a perambulator with his child, accompanied by his wife. Eastern Orthodox priests may marry, but not gain higher ranks. That first step to correcting this situation might be in meeting these gender problems for church leaders, men and women.

Christianity is not the only religion to make women second-class citizens when it comes to participating in religious power; other world

Section Two: Questions About Avatars—Gods Who Become Human

religions do as well. One has to consider, however, whether the selection of gender in Christianity's founding avatar really might still encroach on women's participation in church leadership. It's a difficult question for anyone who would deny women roles of higher leadership in the church.

Given contemporary movements for feminine equality, this problem is rapidly becoming crucial, but recognizing gender-equal leadership qualities will surely solve it. The Catholic Church along with some other more traditional Christian groups and confessions seem to be moving toward such eventual recognition. May it be rapid and soon.

CHAPTER 32

Christianity III: Avatar's People

PEOPLE: THERE IS NO doubt that Yeshua (Jesus) was a Jew; this assertion is made throughout the entire New Testament. When the deity chooses a particular people from whom to be born, this choice as with gender raises major questions. The Jews believe themselves to be a chosen people, a belief found in the Torah (Genesis 12:1–3) where God calls Abraham to "father" nations and makes a covenant with him (Genesis 15:1–6). This sense of being "divinely chosen" has resulted through the centuries in persecution, exile, and even the Holocaust. Anti-Semitism is possibly partially a result, unfortunately, of this claim of "being divinely chosen."

Even the horror of the Nazi Holocaust did not erase such anti-Semitism. It is active in our world today, even in our streets and politics. There still are killings in Jewish synagogues and temples.[124] We must ask ourselves—Why?

History is rife with tales of anti-Semitism, both toward Jews most often, but sometimes, in current history, towards even Arabs and other Semites, although Jews may have the longer history of suffering. One can't help but wonder: What would cause this millennial-long chronicle of Jewish persecution? Why have this particular people been made scapegoats through two millennia of history? Could it be because the Christian avatar, Yeshua, was a Jew? Was it necessary to create a distance from the avatar's followers and those of the avatar's own people who do not acknowledge his divinity? Has that non-acknowledgement of the avatar by some of the avatar's people created an underlying, perhaps unconscious, sense of their outcast status or lower rank in society? Judaism has changed.

Section Two: Questions About Avatars—Gods Who Become Human

The Judaism of today is not that of the time of Yeshua or even of several centuries ago. Judaism has changed across the centuries and is now divided into several groups—*Orthodox* (which includes the Hassidic, coming with the influence of the Baal Shem Tov and others honoring tradition and the non-Hassidic including *Modern Orthodox,* as well as some splinter groups—a few of which claim the Messiah has already come); *Reformed* (arising from a major redefinition of what it means to be a Jew during the late eighteenth and nineteenth centuries, involving modernization); *Conservative* (groups who believed that the Reformed had gone too far but did not want to go as far back as to be Orthodox); and the *Reconstructionists* (a twentieth-century reforming movement that wanted to take Judaism into the future to enhance a newer Jewish civilization), and smaller splinter groups. However, Yeshua probably would not be amazed at the diversity of Judaism of today. Judaism did have multiple divisions in Yeshua's day: Essens, Sadducees, Pharisees, Zealots, Samaritans, and splinter groups.[125]

When an avatar appears in a people, particularly one that understands itself as having been chosen, opportunities arise for those who follow that avatar to disregard the avatar's native people who have not joined them. This disregard sometimes leads to their persecution. Researching this problem, psychiatrists, social psychologists, sociologists of religion and others can aid theologians to find out exactly why anti-Semitism persists and how to end it.

More such research is needed, as well as wide-spread education for tolerance and understanding for all people. One has to wonder why some Christians might persecute Jews when Yeshua or Jesus, claimed as their Savior, was also a Jew.

CHAPTER 33

Christianity IV: Many Messiahs and Many Views

THE NUMBER OF MESSIAH claimants in history is amazing; it seems the list grows longer decade after decade, reinforcing the difficult problems that those who declare themselves to be avatars face in proving their claims.

This is only a partial, very selected list of some of the persons who have claimed or who have been claimed by others to be the Messiah:

Simon Magus (first century) Samaritan;

Dositheos the Samaritan (first century);

Tanchelm of Antwerp (c. 1110);

Ann Lee (1736–1784), a leader of the Shakers;

Bernhard Müller (c. 1799–1834);

John Nichols Thom (1799–1838) sometime in an asylum;

Arnold Potter (1808–1872), Latter Day Saints schismatic;

Hong Xiuquan (1814–1864), Leader of Taiping Uprising;

Jacobina Mentz Maurer (1841?–1872), German-Brazilian;

William W. Davies (1833–1906), Latter Day Saints schismatic;

Cyrus Reed Teed (1839–1908), founder of Koreshanity;

Abd-ru-shin (1875–1941), founder of the Grail Movement;

Father Divine (George Baker) (c. 1880–1965), American church leader;

André Matsoua (1899–1942), Congolese founder of a sect;

Section Two: Questions About Avatars—Gods Who Become Human

Samael Aun Weor (1899-1942), Mexican cult founder;

Ahn Sahng-hong (1918-1985), founder, World Mission Church of God;

Sun Myung Moon (1920-2012), founder of Unification Church;

Yahweh ben Yahweh (1935-2007), founder of the Nation of Yahweh;

Lazlo Toth (1940-2012), smasher of Michelangelo's Pieta;

Wayne Bent (1941-), founder of Lord Our Righteousness Church;

Iesu Matayoshi (1944-), founder of World Economic Community Church;

Jung Myung Seok (1945-), founder of the Providence Church;

Claude Vorilhon (1946-), founded UFO religion—Raël movement;

José Luis de Jesús (1946-2013), founder, Growing in Grace Sect;

Inri Cristo (1948-) of Indaial, Brazil, claimed to be Jesus;

Apollo Quiboloy (1948-), founder of Kingdom of Jesus Christ;

David Icke (1952-) describer of himself as "the Son of God";

Brian David Mitchell (1953-), who said he was a foreordained angel;

David Koresh (1959-1993), leader of Branch Davidians;

Maria Devi Christos (1960-), founder, Great White Brotherhood;

Sergey Torop (1961-), founded Church of the Last Testament;

Alan John Miller (1962-), founded Divine Truth Movement.[126]

This short and very selected list demonstrates how persons have claimed to be the next Messiah by descent, reincarnation or elevation. Each glorified her/himself in a movement, many claiming divinity imitating Yeshua/Jesus.

There are also lists of Muslims who have claimed to be a new messiah or one reincarnated; for these, see the selected list of those claiming to be the *Mahdi* in Chapter 20; Muslims believe the Mahdi is the second coming of Issa (Jesus). Others who do not easily represent Christians or Muslims would make another long list. Some never claimed divine status; a good example is Emperor Haile Selassie of Ethiopia, who was proclaimed Messiah by the Rastafarians.

Comparing the single Christian Messiah to those many avatars in Hinduism, it is interesting to find that only a very few Hindu worshippers seem to claim avatar status, while more in Christianity do so. Most Hindu

Christianity IV: Many Messiahs and Many Views

avatars appear initially as adults with childhoods usually unrecorded. Is the difference in the number of claimants the result of the distinction between the one (Christian) and the many (Hindu) options? Does having only one avatar generate many more claimants while having many avatars might not do so? Do some avatars get lost in the crowd? This question could be investigated by comparative religion scholars.

Christians believe that their proof of the divinity of Yeshua is that he died on a Friday by crucifixion and arose from death the next Sunday. The gospels's canonic descriptions of Yeshua's life and ministry include descriptions of the crucifixion and resurrection in the following passages: Matthew 27:52—28:20; Mark 15:33—16:8; Luke 23:44—24:12; John 19:29—20:18. That the Romans crucified Yeshua raises little doubt; however, the problem of an avatar raised from the dead presents the question of how the incarnated and resurrected body was perceived by those seeing it. Here, the gospel record is not as clear. In Mark 16:14-15, Yeshua "appeared in another form to two of them, [the Disciples] as they walked into the country" and "afterward he appeared to the eleven [Disciples] themselves as they sat at table; and he upbraided them for their unbelief and hardness of heart, because they had not believed those who saw he had risen. [This verse is problematic because it would include Judas, who is recorded to have committed suicide earlier.] The earlier phrase "in another form" underlines the problem of how the resurrected body of Yeshua was perceived, although it does not appear in the next verse "at the table."

In Matthew 27:59-60, Yeshua's dead body is given Jewish funerary rites by the women followers in a tomb donated by Joseph of Arimathea. When the Chief Priests and some Pharisees feared that the disciples might steal the body, they asked Pilate, the Roman Governor, for a Roman guard, but Pilate deferred and said the Temple had its own guards, and those were put at the tomb. After the two Marys went to the tomb (Matthew 28:1-10), they were confronted by an angel who announced the Resurrection; they departed hurriedly and were met by the risen Yeshua, "and they came up and took hold of his feet and worshipped him." There is no comment about "another form" in this reference to the Resurrection, although there are in some others.

In Luke 24:1, the women (Mary Magdalene, Joanna, and Mary, the mother of Yeshua, and the other women with them) had gone to the tomb to anoint Yeshua's body with prepared spices; they couldn't have gone the day before because it was the Sabbath. The women were prepared to do so

Section Two: Questions About Avatars—Gods Who Become Human

because they firmly believed that Yeshua had died. They saw two angels at the open tomb, but no body of Yeshua.

Later, in Luke 24:13–31, two of Yeshua's followers were walking to Emmaus and encountered Yeshua walking with them; however, they did not recognize him until at supper when he took bread, blessed it, and gave it to them; then, they recognized him, but "he vanished out of their sight." When they rushed back to Jerusalem, they were told that the risen Yeshua had appeared to Simon. Then, the risen Yeshua appeared before them and they were frightened, but Yeshua said to them: "Why are you troubled, and do questionings rise in your hearts? See my hands and my feet, for a spirit has no flesh and bones as you see that I have." To assuage their fear, the risen Yeshua asked if they have anything to eat. They gave him some broiled fish, "and he took it and ate before them" (Luke 24:41–43).

This passage argues for not having "another form." but (Luke 24:50–51 reads Yeshua was "carried up into heaven," a passage that might be suggestive of having another bodily form. The account in Luke is not as clear-cut as it is in Matthew, but there is the eating of fish, so Luke seems to stand between Mark's and Matthew's reportage of the resurrected body. The views aren't shared.

In John 20:1–2, Mary Magdalene goes to the tomb alone before dawn and finds the tomb empty. She races to the Disciples to tell them. They come and find burial cloths, but then return home. Mary Magdalene is weeping outside and sees two angels inside the tomb. After talking with them, she turns and sees the risen Yeshua, but she thinks he is the gardener. Yeshua calls her by name, and recognizing him, she responds "Rabboni," which means "teacher" or "rabbi." Then Yeshua says, "Do not hold me, for I have not yet ascended to the Father . . ." (Luke 20:17a). This passage presents a body "in another form" as in Mark. It is apparent the gospels disagree on the bodily form of the resurrected Yeshua.

Granted that the descriptions surrounding the resurrection appear somewhat sketchy and not coherent, one must remember that the persons doing the describing were confused and awe-struck. We must also remember that the narratives were written much later than the crucifixion and resurrection and were not necessarily simultaneous with the each other, so there was time for the confusion and shock to have settled and for the various stories to have had a life of their own, making differences between the narratives.

Christianity IV: Many Messiahs and Many Views

Interpretations from the gospels disagree about the form of the risen Yeshua. They are differently described, so were probably written later after the event. The details of these events reflect the various beliefs that the recorders had.

CHAPTER 34

Christianity V: Humanity vs. Deity

VARIOUS CONTROVERSIES APPEAR IN early Christianity, many of them declared later as heresies. These heresies resulted from early struggles to comprehend the human and divine nature ascribed to Yeshua. Christians argued about the question of how much of Jesus was divine and how much human, a major problem that complicates theology regarding an avatar.

The problem arises when you posit the conviction that only the divine can "save" us humans. Given such a conviction, some might want to preserve the deity of the avatar at the expense of his humanity.

The *Docetists* followed Gnostic concepts in thinking that the divine Christ would not want to be burdened by human flesh, which they assumed was evil through Adam's fall. For them Yeshua was truly divine and *only seemed* to be human, thus, lacking a true body. Docetists believed that Yeshua did not die, simply because a deity cannot die. Docetists favored a passage in the New Testament, Philippians 2:8, which reads: ". . . and [Christ] being found in appearance as a man . . ." For them, Christ, fully divine, only seemed human.[127]

The *Apollinarians* believed that Christ was not equally human and divine. He was a thought to be a person whose flesh existed in divine thought and with God's will. In other words, Christ did not have a human mind or soul and his divinity was in absolute control and made his humanity sacred. Their key passage of scripture was John 1:14: "The Word became flesh," but it did not have a human mind or will.[128] This concept was also Gnostic.

There were also the *Modalists*, also known as *Sibellians*. They believed that the Trinity's nature (Father, Son, Holy Ghost) changed with the role that a particular manifestation was involved in at the time. When God is the Son, He is not the Father. No permanent difference exists between the trinity's three persons; if there were such differences, there would be three deities; their texts are: Exodus 20:3: "You shall have no other gods before me" and "I and the Father are one" John 10:30.[129]

Conversely, some groups believed that Yeshua was very special but not divine. These believers read the four gospels's passages where Yeshua is seen as very much a human being. There were those who took the Yeshua in scripture as human and then decided that he was very special but not divine. One of these groups was called the *Ebionites*, conservative Jews converted to Christianity, who insisted that God must only be One and that Yeshua was just a very knowledgeable and insightful prophet, like those in the Tanakh. Their text could have been I Timothy 2:5: "For there is one God and one mediator between God and men, the man Jesus Christ." For them, Yeshua wasn't divine, only a *man* similar to the Jewish prophets.[130]

Another group labeled heretic was the *Adoptionists*, who felt Yeshua was very extraordinary because God adopted him as a unique son, either at his birth or at his baptism. In his holy adoption, Yeshua was provided with Christ's divine power. In Luke 3:22, at the baptism of Jesus, there is this description: ". . . and the Holy Spirit descended upon him in bodily form, as a dove, and a voice came from heaven, 'Thou art my beloved Son; with thee I am well pleased.'" Other ancient authorities in biblical manuscripts have this line reading: ". . . today I have begotten thee." They did not believe Yeshua was divine until the Holy Spirit adopted him.[131]

The *Arians*, also declared heretical, believed that Christ as the Son was created by God at the beginning of time. Yeshua as the Christ was not perfect like his Creator, although he was the creator's agent in creation of everything; their text: John 1:14: "The Word [is] the only-begotten of the Father."[132]

What was decided after several centuries was that Yeshua was both fully divine and fully human. A heretical group not holding this theological position was called the *Monophysites*, sometimes known as the *Eutychians*. They argued that Yeshua could not have two natures, only one. It was contended that his divine nature was like an ocean overpowering his humanity as if it were only a drop in that divine sea. Their text was Colossians 1:19: "For in him, all the fullness of God was pleased to dwell."[133] This concept waylays Christ's humanity, hampering an ability to be someone who suffers just as others do, since there would be so little humanity with which to suffer as other humans must.

Thus, it seemed a better argument to posit that Yeshua had two "natures" and also two "persons"—one divine and one human, both bound in one body. This was the position of the *Nestorians*, who believed the divine Christ and the human Christ dwelled together in Yeshua. Their text could have been John 2:19: "Destroy this temple and I will raise it up in three days," which implies that although a human Yeshua could have died, the divine would continue, a concept questioning bodily resurrection.[134]

The official position of this tangle of possibilities has been worked on by the Catholic Church for centuries. The solution, reached so far by the Catholic Church's theologians, is the following, found in *The Catholic Encyclopedia*:

THE DOGMA OF THE TRINITY

> The Trinity is the term employed to signify the central doctrine of the *Christian religion*—the *truth* that in the *unity* of the Godhead there are Three Persons, the Father, the Son, and the Holy Spirit, these Three Persons being truly distinct one from another.
>
> Thus, in the words of the Athanasian *Creed*: "the Father is God, the Son is God, and the Holy Spirit is God, and yet there are not three Gods but one God." In this Trinity of Persons the Son is begotten of the Father by an eternal generation, and the Holy Spirit proceeds by an eternal procession from the Father and the Son. Yet, notwithstanding this difference as to origin, the Persons are co-eternal and co-equal: all alike are uncreated and omnipotent.[135]

The Council of Chalcedon (451) was the first to make explicit the nature of the Son in the Trinity. What was argued on was consubstantiation (*homoousios* in Greek) with the Father as all the natures, divine and human, distinct but united in one person. This is termed a *hypostatic union*, perfectly human, perfectly divine.[136]

Thus in Roman Catholic Christianity, Yeshua, the avatar, is a fully divine being, also fully human and part of the Holy Trinity—Father, Son, Holy Spirit. There are not three deities, only one, manifested in different ways but still single. Christian theologians have been working on this conundrum for twenty centuries and it still poses a mystery. It remains as one of the basic problems of Christian theology for non-theologians to work

Christianity V: Humanity vs. Deity

out in their minds. Even persons with theological educations have problems explaining it.

Science can't contribute to this mystery; it seems *solely* theological, one outside of scientific investigation. That admission does not mean that we can avoid utilizing science in studying theology. On the contrary! It only means some questions are beyond human investigation but not our speculation. Science, depending upon facts, proofs, mathematics and experiment, reaches its edges where speculation and theory may extend but knowledge does not yet go. Theology has a more speculative reach than science, but this does not mean that science cannot help in confronting theological conundrums.

CHAPTER 35

Christianity VI: Pro Avatar Reasons

THERE ARE ARGUMENTS THAT posit a positive understanding of the Christian avatar, including those already seen in the Dogma of the Trinity in the last chapter. Admittedly, this concept of the Trinity is really a mystery more than an easily understandable doctrine. Some other interpretations of the questions surrounding the concept of the Incarnation might help balance our understanding of the Christ/Yeshua avatar event.

Two problems exist that an avatar event answers. The first is: What is the deity like, that is, what are God's characteristics and wishes, God's desires and plans for humankind? Were God to become human, it would answer such questions. Granted that records of the events occurring while God becomes human would be scrambled somewhat and sometimes contradictory, primarily because we humans with that ever-present problem of human error recorded such events. Also granted, human error would apply to interpretations of those records after the fact, since these writings also are open to our too human faults.

To be better known to humankind seems an understandable reason for God becoming an avatar, even though the records may be tainted by human error. To take away human error would elevate us humans to a status that negates any need for an avatar and rob us of our freedom of decision.

The second reason for an avatar answers the question: What does God want humankind to be and/or become? Our perception of the avatar shows show us what God is like and also signals what God desires us to become. It shows what God's plan is for us and also for creation. Thus, in one historical event, we learn how God desires us to become as well as what God is like. Those are two major good reasons for an avatar, for an Incarnation.

This reason—to show us what we should strive to be, what we should do with our lives—was presented by Teilhard de Chardin. He argued that Christ represents the "omega point," the final step in human evolution. It is this that we should work to become.[137] So also is the first reason, to understand God better, to know what God is truly like. Throughout the Old Testament (the *Tanakh*), the deity is seen as a creator, an influencer in human affairs sometimes beneficial and sometimes not (the Flood, for example), a maker of covenants with humans, a deliverer of the Hebrews from slavery in Egypt, a sender of prophets and seeker of righteous justice, a loving parent, an answerer to prayer, a restorer of an ancient people. These multiple and sometimes hazy purposes leave us with a desire to know just what God is really like. The Yeshua/Christ event, the Incarnation, provides humans some answers and does so explicitly.

There are some interesting ideas regarding the Incarnation being presented throughout history and they continue today. Some that have recently gained some attention are those of Richard Rohr, whose latest book, *The Universal Christ: How a Forgotten Reality Can Change Everything We See, Hope For, and Believe* (Covergent Books: New York, 2019), has excited his followers and presented a different vision of the Christ event. Father Richard Rohr, a Franciscan (Order of Friars Minor), is a theologian that seems sometimes to nudge towards the Nestorian or Arian heresies but not quite to step over the line into heresy. He likes to remark that Christ is not Jesus's last name. On the contrary, Rohr advocates that the Christ is universal, an attribution of God that is shown in the deity's appearances as Yeshua in events reported in the New Testament; however, the universal Christ's divine attributes can be seen in other religions around the world separate from Christianity. While Yeshua's ministry can be found in the synoptic gospels—Matthew, Mark, Luke—the message of the Universal Christ, according to Rohr, is more easily found in Paul's letters, probably written before the synoptic gospels, in the Gospel of John, and in Revelation. In these, the Universal Christ is seen as God's emanation characterized by a *love* for all persons. Rohr's theology, based on the Universal Christ, is all-inclusive. No one is eliminated; everyone is loved by God.[138]

There are some writers who have not agreed with Rohr or with what some call his almost Nestorian or Arian approaches. In Rohr's favor, it should be noted that some Eastern Orthodox theologians would not find

Section Two: Questions About Avatars—Gods Who Become Human

him heretical, nor do many persons in Western traditions of belief, including Roman Catholics. We should look at some who are questioning whether Rohr is non-heretical, just to balance the argument. "Rohr repeatedly claims that his vision is radical, startling, surprising and new, and that readers might struggle to understand it if they have been raised in traditional Christian faith." The same reviewer, Ian Paul, however, immediately does state: "But he [Rohr] often . . . [claims] that there is little new here, merely a recovery of what writers of the New Testament and their first readers believed, but which the Western church has 'forgotten' or obscured." Questioning Rohr's textual accuracy, Ian Paul continues:

> What is notable . . . is Rohr dislocates these text[s] *both* from their *cultural context,* failing to ask how these words [in the New Testament] might have been understood by either speaker, writer or hearer in the first century, but also ripping them from the wider text itself, ignoring the canonical context, even of immediately surrounding sentences.[139]

Marcia Montenegro wrote a sharper review of Rohr's *The Universal Christ.*

Because Rohr makes a distinction between Jesus and Christ, she claims that this distinction is the major theme of Rohr's book, as Rohr writes on page 23: "Christ is a good and simple metaphor for absolute wholeness, and the integrity of creation. Jesus is the archetypal human just like us (Hebrews 4:15), who shows us what a Full Human might look like if we could live into it (Ephesians 4:12–16)." Her review notes: "Rohr believes everything and everyone will be swept into the final point of perfection drawn to that end by Christ. . . . Rohr's view is that God is now restoring and will restore everything and everyone."[140]

One needs to read Rohr to decide if he is heretical or not. Many do not think so, but some do. As so much in theology, it is a judgment call. One fact remains; Rohr is interesting and gaining an expanding audience.

Richard Rohn is only one of other new theologians who are rethinking the Incarnation. An understanding of the event is open to many interpretations, both orthodox and questionable. Such questions need reexamining and more extended pondering. In science, all is up for reexamination. Should not that also be the case for most areas under question in theology as well? Of course, there are still positions that mark the limits of orthodoxy, but to push at these is good for reinforcing our beliefs and for enriching our theology.

SECTION THREE

Some Recent Scientific Discoveries of Interest and Importance

MANY BREAKTHROUGHS IN SCIENCE have been made over the past century. Reality below atoms has been discovered—quanta, and how these outpace the speed of light. Also discovered was how uncertainty envelopes the universe, smallest to largest. Puzzling forces have been posited—dark matter and dark energy. Fast Radio Bursts stars, flickering like light signals, are another mystery being studied. Do such major developments have relevance for theology?

Physicists find wonders from the tiniest we can comprehend to the outer edges of reality. A quick history of the universe lets us ponder what has been and what might be. Pictures of Black Holes, major advances in understanding them, are being made. Particles of energy, neutrinos highly elusive, are now having laboratories built to study them; these range over 800 miles from Illinois to South Dakota or in the Antarctica with a gigantic square kilometer ice cube.

In this amazing landslide of new scientific discoveries, new ideas have emerged, including those arguing for human survival after death.

CHAPTER 36

What's Below Atoms

IN HIS POSTHUMOUSLY PUBLISHED book, *Brief Answers to the Big Questions*, Stephen Hawking wrote:

> Science is increasingly answering questions that used to be the province of religion. Religion was an early attempt to answer the questions we all ask: why are we here, where did we come from? Long ago, the answer was almost always the same: gods made everything. The world was a scary place, so even people as tough as the Vikings believed in supernatural beings to make sense of natural phenomena like lightning, storms or eclipses.
> Nowadays, science provides better and more consistent answers, but people will always cling to religion, because it gives comfort, and they do not trust or understand science.[141]

A young physicist in Berlin, "a most unlikely scientific revolutionary," "descended from a line of pastors and professors of theology and jurisprudence," was to make a major breakthrough while investigating the physics of cavity radiation. Cavity radiation is obvious to anyone who watches a material—for example, iron—heated to a high temperature. With heat, the material gains energy, becoming red, then yellow, then white from the heat, emitting a bright light as it does. The photons from the material as it heats gain higher frequency, which provide the changes in color of the light—the higher the frequency, the brighter the light. Light is a form of radiation. This breakthrough scientist was Max Planck. Noting this change in frequency, Planck discovered his physical law: radiation is directly related to frequency—the higher the frequency, the greater the radiation. Light is

Section Three: Some Recent Scientific Discoveries of Interest and Importance

composed of photons, a form of energy. Planck's Law ($E = \hbar v$) states that E (energy) "is composed of a very definite number of equal finite packets" which Planck termed *quanta* [$\hbar$] for it meant that energy itself could be *quantified*.[142] Beneath the level of atoms lie quarks, which are made up of the energy particle fields of quanta, the latter a level that is the smallest yet found. This level exists at an accurate measurement of (10^{-35}).[143]

In 1905, a half-decade after Planck's discovery, Einstein wrote "that Planck's law of radiation only makes sense if radiation itself is thought to be composed of discreet packets of energy which he called light-quanta."[144]

Planck's discovery was the beginning of a revolution in physics termed quantum mechanics. The energy and frequency of quanta are higher for ultraviolet and X–rays than for infrared or visible light. The differences signal that there exists a spectrum of energy, which, when stimulated, produces particles measured by their frequency, that is, their rates of vibration. The quanta are in waves, as de Broglie noted, but can only be identified by stimulated particles in waves. He was able to show that the velocity of such matter waves would be greater than the speed of light.[145]

An important thought experiment (*Gedankenexperiment*) presented by Einstein during the Fifth Solvay Conference at Brussels in October 1927 expanded the theory of quantum mechanics. He imagined a source of photons in a beam hitting a diffracting barrier with *one* slit in it. The photons then hit a second sheet (possibly of photographic paper) and are recorded there. The result is only one vertical line matching the vertical slit in the barrier. Unlike the one slit barrier, another with two slits produces a much different pattern, with several lines not only corresponding to the two slits but also recording several other lines. This is because waves have highs and lows, so photons, being quanta, can interfere with each other.[146]

Experiments demonstrate that there is a collapse of the wave function, which implies a peculiar action at a distance. The photons somehow appear to change the physical state of the system from the point where the measurement is actually recorded. The photons seem not to obey rules, for they interfere with each other. Shown on the second sheet behind the double-slit barrier experiment is an interference pattern where particles interfere with other particle's paths.[147] This interesting phenomenon would lead to the discovery of quantum entanglement, where entangled quanta separated by vast distances react when the other entangled with it receives an effect and the other does not, so that the reaction causes the same outcome to happen simultaneously to the second *supposedly* unaffected particle. Here

What's Below Atoms

is a thought experiment. Imagine a laser shown onto a prism point so that the laser beam is split where it goes to the right and to the left. A laser is a single photon beam. On the left, a distance from a splitting prism receiving the laser beam is a mirror placed at a 45-degree angle to the beam so that the left split beam is diverted to be parallel to the originating beam prior to hitting the prism. On the right there is no mirror; however, when the beam is shown hitting the mirror on the left, the beam on the right will also take the same angle as the one on the left, but without the mirror. This phenomenon was termed by Joseph Bell, its discoverer, as quantum entanglement, "where two parts of a particle can retain a 'spooky' connection, even when very far apart."[148]

Quantum entanglements present an open door for theologians to enter and explore phenomena that may have major bearings on our theology. What is entangled, and what is not? Most importantly, why does entanglement exist?

Another interesting reality is Heisenberg's Uncertainty Principle. Stephen Hawking explained Werner Heisenberg's very important discovery thus:

> There seems to be a certain level of randomness or uncertainty in nature that cannot be removed however good our theories. It can be summed up in the Uncertainty Principle that was proposed by the German scientist Werner Heisenberg. One cannot accurately predict both the position and the speed of a particle. The more accurately the position is predicted, the less accurately you will be able to predict the speed, and vice versa.[149]

This problem of uncertainty is inherent at the quantum level and thus throughout all reality. Please carefully note: Uncertainty is locked into reality. As we look at the night sky and consider the magnificence of space, we too often forget that space/time between the stars is not empty; on the contrary, it is filled with energy fields.

> The effect of these ... virtual particles in empty space can be demonstrated in the laboratory through what is called the Casimir effect, discovered in 1948 by Dutch physicist Hendrik Casimir. Two closely spaced metal plates will actually be pushed closer together due to the fact that the pressure from virtual photons in the gap between the plates no longer balances pressure of virtual photons outside the gaps.[150]

Section Three: Some Recent Scientific Discoveries of Interest and Importance

Besides Quantum Entanglement and the Uncertainty Principle, there are also the problems of the unknown energies and materials making up our universe. Not only is space/time far from empty; it is filled with energy fields and a somewhat small amount of matter, as well as a lot of "dark matter" and "dark energy."

At the beginning of 2020, NASA's Jet Propulsion Laboratory announced that they had "imaged" small clumps of dark matter "using the Hubble Space Telescope and a new observing technique." Dark matter was proven to exist.[151]

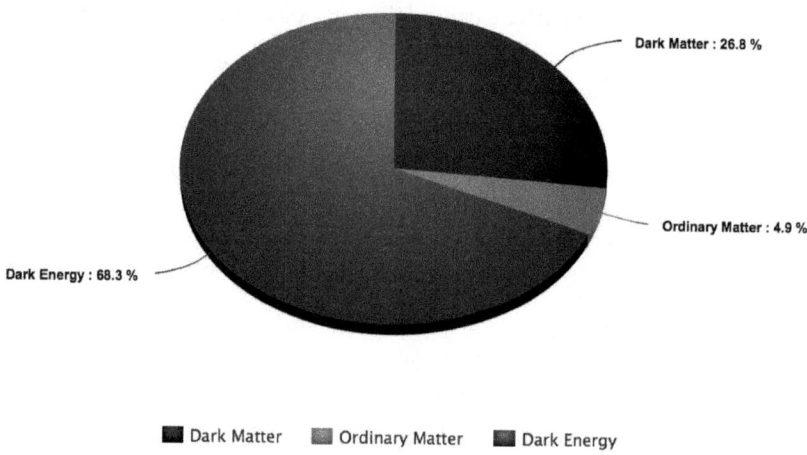

Mass–energy-pie-chart. Berkeley Lab. Glen Roberts Jr. "3 Known and 3 Unknowns about Dark Matter," May 24, 2016

These currently opened doors in science might allow us to explore areas where science and theology could share information. The level of random uncertainty in the universe with quantum entanglement, dark energy and dark matter and a multitude of other universal mysteries provide fields for mutual discussions. Creation's magnificence mirrors its Maker.

CHAPTER 37

A Word of Caution About Doors

The "doors" mentioned in the last chapter are suggested points for theologians to begin their inquiries; however, not all questions presently still unsolved in science become "open doors." We need to realize the difference between those where we can enter and those where we need to allow time to wait for science to unpack more of the universe's mysteries.

An intriguing problem of cosmology would serve as one example—the increasing speed of the galaxies moving away from each other. Edward Hubble, Mount Wilson astronomer, discovered in 1929 that the universe is expanding. The problem with this expansion is that it seems not to be uniform over time; the expansion is about "9 percent" faster than the accepted current theory estimates. Dennis Overby, at Johns Hopkins, notes:

> But this slight-sounding discrepancy has intrigued astronomers, who think it might be revealing something new about the universe. And so, for the last couple of years, they have been gathering in workshops and conferences to search for a mistake or loophole in their previous measurements and calculations, so far to no avail.[152]

A group at Johns Hopkins University has proposed that the problem might be solved by positing an unknown energy force being switched on when the universe was approximately only 100,000 years old, a very early period of universe history; then after another 100,000 years, the energy source shut off. The extra early boost gave the universe's expansion the nine percent extra velocity that would solve the problem.[153] The Johns Hopkins theory is only one of several that have been proposed in the past several years at workshops and conferences of concerned cosmologists. Lisa Randall,

Section Three: Some Recent Scientific Discoveries of Interest and Importance

a cosmological theorist at Harvard University, noted, "If we're going to be serious about cosmology, this is the kind of thing we have to be able to take seriously." Other scientists propose that the extra speed of the galaxies moving away from each other might be understood by positing existence of some previously undiscovered subatomic particles. These particles are not the same as the Johns Hopkins proposed energy. Others also caution that there exists a source already proposed—"dark energy"—creating the expansion.[154]

Another approach suggests there is a new kind of neutrino—a fourth type—that could possibly provide answers. Still another proposal suggests that there are fields of anti-gravitational energy, an idea arising from "String Theory" that posits elementary reality is made of very minute strings. These fields of strings—termed "quintessence"—might operate by resisting gravity and then reversing their effect. Some teams working on this theory use the term "axions" for such hypothetical particles. Were the axions active in the early years of the universe, they could have been the right energy for the speed-up in the Hubble constant of galactic speed. Axion theorists refer sometimes to this force as "early dark energy."[155]

Michael Turner, cosmologist at the University of Chicago, who organized a recent discussion of the galaxies speed questions said, "Indeed, all of this is going over all our heads. We are confused and hoping that the confusion will lead to something good."[156]

None of these proposals has received a majority of cosmologists' support or recognition; what is finally decided as the cause will radically change our understanding of the how the universe began and now operates.

Important in this debate is that it is unresolved, unlike other scientific theories, such as Heisenberg's Uncertainty Principle or various aspects of quantum mechanics such as quantum entanglement and superposition, which most scientists now agree on. Scholars in theology need to be aware that the problem of galaxy speed increase would not make a good "open door" for further study yet.

CHAPTER 38

FRBs: An Example of a Trap

FRBs—FAST RADIO BURSTS—ARE RADIO waves discovered by radio astronomers. They're very short, often only milliseconds, but unbelievably strong, one producing more energy in that millisecond than our Sun would produce in an entire day. First found in 2007, FRBs were discovered by an undergraduate, David Narkevic at West Virginia University, when he was looking for pulsar flashes from neutron stars in some older photographic plates. Pulsars form when stars create supernovas and then collapse into a neutron star. These neutron star pulsars spin very fast, sometimes revolving in seconds, sending out bursts of energy as they do; these bursts sweep across the universe like light beams from a lighthouse.[157]

At first, many radio astronomers rejected the idea that these rapid energy bursts were something different—a new type of radio signal—but soon others were found. A major discovery was made in 2017 when gravitational waves, major ripples in space-time, resulted from the collision of two neutron stars. These waves provided the information regarding the neutron stars's masses "right before the crash which scientists have used to place new limitations on the properties and possible compositions of all neutron stars."[158] Measurements from the FRBs are possible by timing the waves of the electromagnetic field; as energy increases in that spectrum, the wavelength decreases. Radio waves are at the lower end of this electromagnetic spectrum; AM waves are slower than FM. The less energetic radio waves bump into matter in space, slowing them down. Scientists measure the slow radio waves and because they arrive later than the higher ones, which do not bump into matter, the distance to the source of the slower waves can

Section Three: Some Recent Scientific Discoveries of Interest and Importance

be calculated when compared to the arrival time of the more rapid waves. The time delay between frequencies, what is called the dispersion measure (DM), provides the distance to the source.[159]

A burst from our galaxy would possibly measure a DM of 30, while one from the Magellanic Clouds outside our galaxy would measure more than 200. One FRB discovered earlier had a DM of 790, a far reach into the universe. These FRBs have to be caused by very high-energy sources, but even today, there are differing theories as to what causes them. Victoria Kaspi, McGill University, carefully noted: "None of the models exist without major problems."[160]

One FRB, 121102 (12 representing the year 2012, 11 November, and 02 the day) seemed different, primarily because it is a repeater. Most FRBs burst only once and even with persistent observations do not do so again. However, 121102 will be quiet "for weeks or months at a time, and then it will burst several times a day. There is no pattern." Observations from around the world have revealed that this repeater's home appears to be "a nondescript dwarf galaxy 3 million light-years away, . . . the size of the Large Magellanic Cloud, some 10 percent as big as the Milky Way." This discovery was a surprise. Some experts suggested that FRBs might be a particular type of a neutron star termed a magnetar, one with extremely strong magnetic fields. Emily Pestroff, a radio astronomer at the University of Amsterdam, stated, "Finding more FRBs is the most urgent goal at the moment. We just don't have enough information of where they're coming from."[161]

Recent findings on FRBs in the January (2019) issue of *Nature* are that astronomers are finally beginning to understand the mystery of FRB 121102, the only then known repeating FRB. This FRB is thought to be near a massive black hole, a supernova remnant, which has a gigantic magnetized cloud of gas and dust or possibly a neutron star within one of these extreme locations. These discoveries do not explain the FRB's ultimate pulsating causes, but they do offer some possibilities for understanding FRBs that repeatedly pulsate. Research on FRBs continues and while finding more repeaters, still is concentrated on finding more answers.[162]

FRBs represent a potential trap door for some unsuspecting theologians to try to open. They are still not fully understood, and the theories for them are not firmly established. Some skeptical preachers might be tempted to say that these are messages from the deity, which should be decoded and thus someone might devote a life to a wasted effort. Were God wanting to communicate, this would be a very obtuse method unlike anything else in history. One might believe that these flashes are signals from alien beings, attempting to communicate. Were the aliens using FRBs to do so, they would have few problems with space travel or with creating a much clearer form of cross-universe communication, due to their ability to harness such extremely, unbelievably high energy.

These three possibilities for FRBs serve as potential traps for theological investigation. At these possible scientific doors, non-scientists should patiently wait for more and clearer answers from a majority of astronomers working on FRBs.

There are many discoveries in science that provide material for theologians to work with in gaining insight into finding the "fingerprints" of the universe's Maker. There's enough so that there is no need to rush to the latest and most intriguing discoveries just because they make headlines.

Chapter 39

Us, the Stars and Their Energy

CARL SAGAN OFTEN REMARKED, "The Cosmos is within us. We are made of star-stuff. We are a way for the universe to know itself."[163] Other cosmologists have been more specific; for example, Lawrence M. Krauss in his book, *A Universe from Nothing: Why There is Something Rather Than Nothing*, he noted:

> The amazing thing is that every atom in your body came from a star that exploded. And, the atoms in your left hand probably came from a different star than your right hand. It really is the most poetic thing I know about physics. You are all stardust. You wouldn't be here if stars hadn't exploded, because the elements—the carbon, nitrogen, oxygen, iron, all the things that matter for evolution—weren't created at the beginning of time. They were created in the *nuclear* furnaces of stars, and the only way they could get into your body is if those stars were kind enough to explode... The stars died so you could be here today.[164]

You, dear reader, are a walking, talking, wondering bundle of stardust, and that fact needs to be acknowledged by theologians who overlook what science has to offer in understanding who we really are and why. It makes sense that God used the universe to create us. The universe is said to be created *ex nihilo*, that is, made from nothing, but not us humans. Science is very clear on this: *we evolved*, ultimately from the elements in stardust.

These elements you are composed of carry information. Any atom of an element carries information. For example, an atom of sodium (Na) has the ability to combine with an atom of chloride (Cl), producing a molecule

Us, the Stars and Their Energy

(NaCl). These molecules are in your kitchen in the saltshaker. Some elements can combine with others but not all with all. There is information in each atom that allows a combination or not, depending on what else is present. These molecules break down into atoms, which also carry information.

Below the atom in size is the quark. Quarks are elementary subatomic particles. Protons and neutrons, composed of quarks, are two of the constituents that make up an atom's nucleus. There are six types of quarks, called "flavors," different from each other by mass and charge. Quarks cannot be split into anything smaller,[165] although quanta are smaller and more fundamental—tiny particles of *energy*, but notice, not *matter*. Einstein's equation separates the two: ($E = mc^2$). The E is energy, m is matter, and c is the speed of light, which is squared. The six flavors of quarks are: *up/down, strange/charmed, bottom/top*. Scientists refer to quark "colors," which are only a way of labeling them, because quarks are smaller than visible light's (photons) wavelength. For example, a proton is composed of three quarks with the fundamental colors of *blue, red*, and *green*; so is a neutron, but the difference is that the proton has a quark that is *two up and one down* while the neutron has a *two down and one up*. For each quark, there is an antiquark. Particles also have another quality; ". . . everything in the universe, including light and gravity, can be described in terms of particles." These particles have a property called "spin." You might be thinking that this is too detailed for gaining an insight into a theological concept; however, if every particle in the universe has spin, it does open up some interest. For every particle, there is an antiparticle. If they meet, they annihilate. That fact could be of interest in theology. Stephen Hawking observed:

> All the known particles in the universe can be divided into two groups: particles with a spin ½, which make up the matter of the universe, and particles of spin 0, 1, and 2, which . . . give rise to forces between the matter particles.[166]

These forces are crucial in physics, for they are thought to explain every action. The first is *gravity* (including space and time), which is the weakest of these four forces, but it is always attractive and can act over very long distances, unlike the others which have either actions short distanced or may be attractive or repulsive, depending upon the occasion. Again, Hawking explains: "In the quantum mechanical way of looking at the gravitational field, the force between two matter particles is pictured as being carried by a particle of spin 2 called the *graviton*. This has no mass of its own, so the force that it carries is long range."[167]

Section Three: Some Recent Scientific Discoveries of Interest and Importance

The next force is the *electromagnetic;* it influences quarks and electrons, effecting particles that are charged electrically. To compare the two forces, the force between two electrons is 10^{42} times greater than that of the graviton. In this force, as most people know, there are two types of electrical charge, positive and negative, where opposites attract and similar repel. Think of a magnet. This force, the electromagnetic, allows *electrons* (negative) to orbit the atomic nucleus composed of *protons* (positive) and *neutrons* (neither – nor +). There is a variation in electrical charge in each.[168]

The third force is the *weak nuclear*. It causes radioactivity and effects particles having matter and spin of ½, but not spin of 0, 1, or 2, that is, particles such as gravitons and protons. Adbus Salam at Imperial College, London, and Steven Weinberg at Harvard University both advanced theories that merged the weak nuclear force with the electromagnetic force. They did so by adding a new concept—"spontaneous symmetry breaking," that is, "what appears as a number of completely different particles at low energies are, in fact, found to be all the same type of particle, only in different states." At high energy levels, the particles appear similar, but at lower energy levels, they can be differentiated. With this idea and further research, it was realized that the two forces, electromagnetic and weak nuclear, could be melded.[169]

The fourth force is the *strong nuclear,* which holds the quarks of the *proton* and *neutron* together. What carries this force is another spin of one particle called a *gluon*. This force exhibits confinement, which prevents the viewing of an isolated gluon or isolated quark. This force also exhibits "asymptomatic freedom." At lower energies, quarks and gluons cannot be isolated; however, at the much higher energies found in larger particle accelerators, the strong nuclear force becomes weaker and then the quarks and gluons begin to behave similarly to free particles. This finding allows theorists to begin formulating a possible Grand Unified Theory or GUT, a theory that would combine all four forces into one. Such a theory has not been completely hammered out yet, but physicists are working on it, proposing that since the strong nuclear force gets weaker at higher energies and the electromagnetic and weak nuclear forces get stronger at higher energies, then there *might* be a Grand Unification Theory (GUT), combining all three forces: electromagnetic, weak nuclear and strong nuclear into one, a theory of a single force. Unfortunately, an accelerator capable of producing such energies would "have to be as big as the Solar System."[170]

Us, the Stars and Their Energy

At molecular, atomic, and quark levels, each level carries information for functioning that is responsive to one of the four major forces. Thus, *information is carried by mass and energy.* The information in the universe is not just out there in space, it is also it inside of you, making you who you are. From the smallest bits of energy to the most gigantic of galaxies, there is information at work. This very important fact will become crucial later, particularly as a possible answer to a major question in theology. What happens to us when we die?

Chapter 40

Possible Answers to Questions

WE NEED TO BACK up a moment and tackle some major cosmic questions. These discoveries have potential to present possible insights later when examined theologically. This becomes apparent when we realize that our understanding of the history of the cosmos, particularly its early stages, is relatively scant. What physicists have recently theorized seems truly amazing.

Charles Bennett of Johns Hopkins University and Michael S. Turner of the University of Chicago explained the current theories of cosmic history and other questions in *National Geographic*: "*Cosmic Questions*":

> In the twentieth century the universe became a story—a scientific one. It had always been seen as static and eternal. Then astronomers observed other galaxies flying away from ours, and Einstein's general relativity theory implied space itself was expanding—which meant the universe had once been denser. What had seemed eternal now had a beginning and an end. What beginning? What end? Those questions are still open.[171]

The first question Bennett and Turner answer is: "*What Is Our Universe Made Of?*" and their answer is:

> Stars, dust and gas—the stuff we can discern—make up less that 5 percent of the universe. Their gravity can't account for how galaxies hold together.
>
> Scientists figure about 24 percent of the universe is a mysterious dark matter—perhaps exotic particles formed right after inflation. The rest is dark energy, an unknown energy field or property

Possible Answers to Questions

of space that counteracts gravity, providing an explanation for observations that the expansion of space is accelerating.[172]

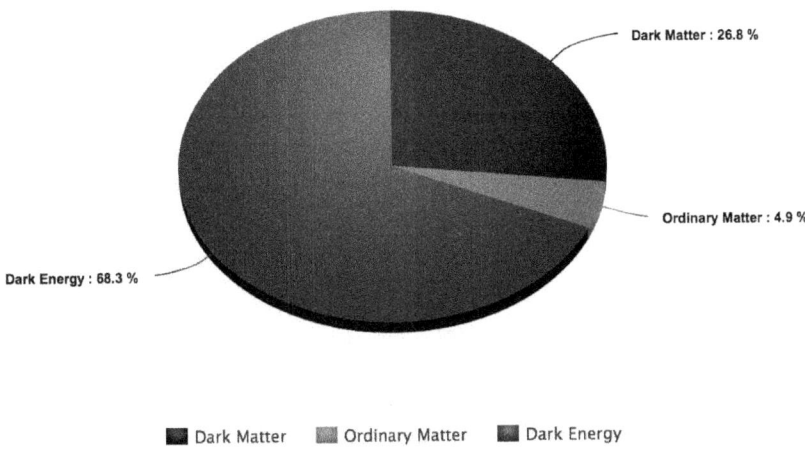

Mass–energy-pie-chart. Berkeley Lab. Glen Roberts Jr. "3 Known and 3 Unknowns about Dark Matter," May 24, 2016

In answering the question of *"How Did Our Universe Begin?"* Bennett and Turner presented the following scenario. About 13.8 billion years ago, there was "an unimaginably hot dense point" perhaps a "billionth the size of a nuclear particle" that blew-up, "expanding radically." This Big Bang explosion, "in far less than a nanosecond," creates a repulsive energy "to visible size," filling it "with a soup of subatomic particles called quarks." Estimates are that this event was approximately "10^{-32} milliseconds" and that growth was from "infinitesimal to golf ball" size. Then, from ".01 milliseconds to 0.1 trillionth present size" of the universe, space (width) expands and so does time (speed). The universe cools, and "quarks clump into protons and neutrons, the building blocks of atomic nuclei. Perhaps dark matter forms." As cooling continues, "the lightest nuclei of hydrogen and helium arise. A thick fog of particles blocks all light." Time is between ".01 to 200 seconds" and the universe is one billionth its present size. "As electrons begin orbiting nuclei, creating atoms, the glow from our infant universe is unveiled. This light is as far back as our instruments can see." The universe is about "380,000 years" old and about " .0009 present size." The next period of our universe's history is sometimes termed the "dark ages" for the reason that for "300 million years this cosmic background radiation is the only light." During this period, "clumps of matter that will

Section Three: Some Recent Scientific Discoveries of Interest and Importance

become galaxies glow brightest." It is estimated that this time is "380,000 to 300 million years" since the Big Bang, and the universe has expanded from ".0009 to 0.1 present size." When "gravity wins," the "dense gas clouds collapse under their own gravity—and that of dark matter—to eventually form galaxies and stars" and then "nuclear fusion lights up the stars." This time is about "300 million years" and the universe is " 0.1 present size." "After being slowed for billions of years by gravity, cosmic expansion accelerates again. The culprit: dark energy. Its nature: unclear." Time is "10 billion years" and size is now " .77 percent." "Today the universe continues to expand, becoming ever less dense. As a result, fewer new stars and galaxies are forming." Time is "13.8 billion years" and the universe is its "present size."[173]

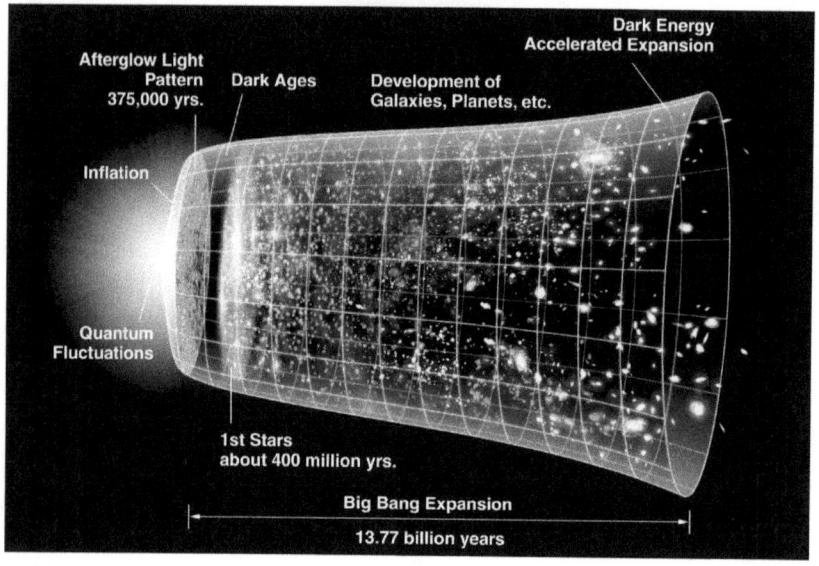

Chronology of the universe

This very condensed history of our universe leaves us with many unanswered questions; these are raised by Bennett and Turner as questions for which the answers, we can hope, are still forthcoming. A few of these questions are: *"What is the shape of the universe?"* and *"How will it end?"* as well as *"Do we live in a multiverse?"* For the first question, shape, they propose three answers from different theories: a sphere, a saddle, and flat. For the second, the end, they propose three theoretical propositions: a "big crunch" where the inflation ends and gravity conflates to another initial point of energy similar to the initial source—the Big Bang; the "big rip" where the "dark energy will trigger a big rip that shreds everything," and "infinite expansion," where the universe will "expand for hundreds of billions of years, long after all stars have died."[174]

One has to ask: Isn't the eventual end of the universe (if there is one) really also a theological question? Must theologians unwittingly abandon this question to the physicists? Is it only we humans that must seek to know more about what will happen? Surely it is important for theologians to study the possible end of humankind. If we ever go to the other galaxies, perhaps we might find some answers to these fundamental questions.

We humans began in trees, moved to caves, slowly covered the Earth, and now find ourselves on a planet in an immense universe, the observed possible edges over 47 billion light years away. We left the trees, then the caves. Why not now also the planet we live on? There may be ways for us to reach for the stars.

That expedition into the galaxy and then the universe could demand us to be theologically as well as scientifically cognizant of the potential problems and benefits of our discoveries. For example, interracial struggles would seem minor when compared to interspecies conflict.

CHAPER 41

Gravitational Waves to the Rescue

GRAVITATIONAL WAVES ARE DISTORTIONS of space/time, surging "ripples in the fabric of the universe." When two neutron stars collided 130 million years ago, "a gravitational wave rippled across the universe" and "the fabric of space-time. Light from the cataclysm followed seconds later." The wave reached Italy's gravitational waves detector, Advanced Virgo (AVD), and then LIGO (Laser Interferometer Gravitational-wave Observatory) in the United States. LIGO had earlier measured two black holes in collision, initiating the era of astronomy aided by gravitational wave reception. These gravitational waves allowed astronomers to study several areas of inquiry.[175]

The first of these areas is *black holes*, specifically the first black holes that have been posited by theorists to have formed in the beginning of the universe, possibly over 13 billion years ago, about 690 million years after inflation; however, some theorists argue that some were created earlier, "a fraction of a second of the Big Bang." If they were created then, these nascent black holes remain only conjectural and unknowable; however, the new information coming from studying gravitational waves might confirm these very earliest black holes. Such knowledge will aid our growing knowledge of the universe's history. Savvas Koushiappas of Brown University and Avi Loeb of Harvard University created a method for searching for these earliest black holes using the gravitational waves created by their collisions. These earliest black holes were a problem, for the consensus was that black holes formed from stars, and stars had not yet formed at that time in the growth of the universe. Star-based black holes could not have formed and then collided until at least 67 million years after the Big Bang.[176]

Were LIGO to find gravitational waves from black hole collisions happening before the birth of stars, two possibilities would exist: one, there were these primordial black holes near the birth of the universe, or two, the standard proposed history of the universe was faulty. Were the first proposal true, then Koushiappas and Loeb have determined that primordial black holes could make up some of the universe's still-unexplained dark matter, so the finding could offer a partial solution to one of astronomy's biggest mysteries. Unfortunately, it seems it did not supply that solution.[177]

The second area where gravitational waves come to aid current theory is in the area of "strange matter." One place to look is in neutron stars, what is "left over after violent deaths of stars too small to become black holes." In a neutron star, density is "roughly 100 trillion times greater than liquid water" because the star's original collection of atoms had "broken down into neutrons, protons and electrons" which were then "squeezed together to form more neutrons"—"an entity made up of nothing but neutrons."[178]

In this squeezed mass, "the neutrons in the dense cores . . . revert to their basic constituents," so the quarks are in a "precariously balanced dynamo" adding strange quarks. "It just takes a tiny bit of energy to convert an up or down quark into a strange quark," and this process converts other quarks into strange quarks, converting the entire neutron star into a strange matter star," according to Pedro Moraes, astrophysicist at Brazil's National Institute for Space Research. Were a neutron star and strange star to merge, the frequency of the gravitational waves, according to Moraes, "will be higher when the system contains one strange star and higher still in the case of a strange star binary." Being smaller, strange stars circle more rapidly, "increasing both the strength and the frequency of the gravitational wave emissions," proving that strange stars exist and indicating "whether strange matter is really the universe's most stable form of matter." Another insight would be whether strange matter really "is the most stable form of matter, capable of turning everything it touches into more strange matter."[179]

Another set of questions that study of gravitational waves would enlighten would be the existence of extra dimensions. Theodore Kaluza, a German mathematician, suggested to Einstein [in 1919] a way of combining gravity and electromagnetism into a single, cohesive force—a longtime goal of physics, but it required five dimensions. String theory in the 1980s went even further, positing the existence of *six* additional tiny and unseen

Section Three: Some Recent Scientific Discoveries of Interest and Importance

dimensions in an attempt to unify the particles and four known forces of nature into a single framework.

No extra dimensions have yet been found evidentially, but CERN physicist David Andriot and his colleague, Gustavo Lucena Gómez, formerly at Max Planck Institute, say these dimensions might be concealed within gravitational wave ripples. Such is possible because the gravitational waves shrink and stretch space-time through their movement, causing a flutter termed "a breathing mode," the signal changing as if it were in or out.[180]

There are three larger gravitational wave observatories, the already mentioned LIGO and the European Virgo Interferometer, and the new Japanese KAGRA gravity wave telescope. Were these research centers to detect the aforesaid mode, Andriot states, it could, if positive, be evidence for extra dimensions, and if negative, would, according to Andriot, tell us "gravity doesn't behave the way we think it ought to." Either finding would demand a redefinition of physics theories.[181]

Another area where gravitational waves could help astrophysicists is regarding echoes, which might be carried by these waves. In the instance of a black hole, there is a question of whether surrounding the *event horizon*—the band where the light is being absorbed—there is a firewall.[182] When there is a set of gravitational waves from a collision, it is possible that the sounds incorporated into the waves would produce echoes. An analysis of such possible echoes could suggest a firewall, which would be the cause of the sound to bounce back and thus produce an echo. Vitor Cardoso of the Instituto Superior Técnico in Lisbon suggests that this would possibly indicate a firewall's existence. Niayesh Afshordi at the University of Waterloo and Perimeter Institute suggested that such echoes exist in the data from the first three detections at LIGO. Afshordi and many others are eagerly awaiting any further evidence of future gravitational waves coming from LIGO, Virgo, and KAGRA.[183]

Another area where gravitational waves could aid astrophysicists is determining differences between black holes and wormholes. Ludwig Flamm, a German physicist, the year after Einstein published his equations for his theory of general relativity, found in them the probability for what would be described as wormholes, small tunnels "connecting two different parts of the universe, or our universe and another." Einstein termed them "bridges."[184]

The possibility has been raised that what are some entities known as black holes could instead be wormholes. Vitor Cardoso and his colleagues in 2016 found that wormholes—which would be massive and compact as black holes, but lacking an event horizon—could emit the same kind of gravitational echoes as a firewall-encased black hole. Researchers at Katholieke Universiteit Leuven in Belgium reached the same conclusion in 2018. Thomas Hertog, a former student of Stephen Hawking, now at Katholieke Universiteit Leuven, noted, "Wormholes are modifications of black holes." They are different solutions to the same equations. Evidence for black holes is much stronger by far than for wormholes. Further study of gravitational waves may provide evidence for studying wormholes, if they happen to exist.[185]

Research from the analysis of gravitational waves has been a new area in astrophysics, and the questions it raises are very important. They are fascinating for theologians to look at for their understanding of how the universe with its colliding neutron stars, dark matter and dark energy, stars making gravitational waves as well as the fields of subatomic particles might show us some possible "fingerprints" of the universe's Creator. Finding these "fingerprints" is a goal for both science and theology.

Chapter 42

Visible Proof of Black Holes

The existence of black holes can no longer be conjecture. April 10, 2019, it was announced that an image of a black hole had been successfully made. "The picture shows a halo of dust and gas, tracing the outline of a colossal black hole, at the heart of Messier 87 galaxy, 55 million light years from Earth." This first in astronomy history was accomplished by the Event Horizon Telescope (EHT), "eight radio telescopes spanning locations from Antarctica to Spain and Chile" and "involving more than 200 scientists." The accretion disk surrounding the black hole and the event horizon of the black hole are readily seen. The event horizon is where light itself is captured by gravity. The picture shows an area "where reality is so fierce that reality as we know it is distorted beyond recognition." "The sheer volume of the data generated was also unprecedented—in one night the ETH generated enough data to fill a ton of hard drives."[186]

The entire procedure would not have been possible without the major contribution by Katie Bouman of California Institute of Technology, who, while studying at MIT, came up with the key algorithm, a computation necessary to have each of the telescopes stitched together for data collected from across the entire worldwide EHT network. She had to work out the calculation after studying half a ton of hard drives at MIT's Haystack Observatory. It was a solution to "an unprecedented computational challenge."[187]

Visible Proof of Black Holes

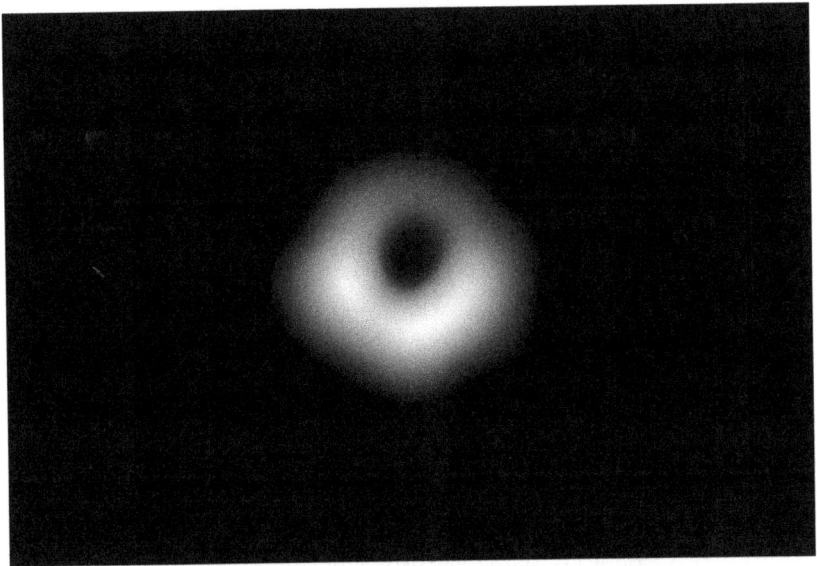

NASA, JPL, California Institute of Technology, April 19, 2019. Ota Lutz, "How Scientists Captured the First Image of a Black Hole."

Seeing a black hole allows scientists to study the composition and functioning of these mysteries of the universe. What we shall see in later chapters is the question of whether information can survive in a black hole, a major question for physics. This accomplishment of the photograph is an excellent example of why theologians must wait for breakthroughs prior to opening doors; once new information is available, they should begin asking how relevant it is to theological insights. Black Holes capture the imaginations of theologians, possibly causing them to question why God created such things and for what purpose.

Chapter 43

Some More Advances in Science

SCIENTISTS HAVE SEEN THE universe through many media, first light, which is really photons, but lately also extensions across the electromagnetic spectrum such as infrared, X-rays, and even gamma rays. Radio waves have also been used from the lower end of the electromagnetic spectrum. Up until now, there has not been an ability to use neutrinos, but that has now been solved. Two papers reported in *Science* (July 2018) report astronomers can now also "observe" with neutrinos.[188]

Neutrinos interact very weakly with matter. Neil DeGrasse Tyson noted:

> The copious flux of neutrinos from the Sun—two neutrinos for every helium nucleus fused from hydrogen in the Sun's thermonuclear core—exit the Sun unfazed by the Sun itself, travel through the vacuum of space at nearly the speed of light, then pass though Earth as though it does not exist. The tally: night and day, a hundred billion neutrinos from the Sun pass through each thumbnail patch of your body, every second, without a trace of interaction with your body's atoms.[189]
>
> In an atom, protons (positive +) and neutrons (neutral 0) are surrounded by electrons (negative -). When a proton snares an electron (electron capture), another *neutron* is formed, but a *neutrino*, a particle, is released. For example, if a beryllium atom (*Be* atomic number 4) has a proton capture of an electron, beryllium's atomic number is reduced to 3, the atomic number of lithium (*Li* 3) and it becomes an entirely different element. *Be* has four electrons, four protons, and three neutrons while *Li* has three electrons, three protons, four neutrons (result of the merger) and emits a neutrino particle, *an electron neutrino* (μe). Other

Some More Advances in Science

neutrinos result from decay: muon and tau neutrinos, muons and taus being particles found in atoms. All of these neutrinos have opposite partners—antineutrinos. Neutrinos interact weakly with other particles; thus, it very difficult to detect neutrinos making them most difficult to study. The good news is that several neutrino observatories have been or are being built.[190]

One of the most fascinating of these new observatories is called IceCube in Antarctica, which uses a cubic kilometer of ice to capture neutrinos. Darren Grant, astroparticle physicist at the University of Alberta, working at the IceCube neutrino-capturing laboratory, commented:

> The field of neutrino astronomy has become a reality. For decades it has been a dream of many to harness high-energy neutrinos as one of nature's ideal astronomical messengers. This detection has opened for us a new window with which to view the universe, much the same as the discovery of gravitational waves did recently.[191]

Another major neutrino project is being built by Fermilab (just west of Chicago in Batavia, Illinois) with the Sanford Underground Research Facility (in Lead, South Dakota) in the old Homestake Mine; it is called the Deep Underground Neutrino Experiment (DUNE), set to begin in 2026. DUNE will have a new particle accelerator at Fermilab, where a cycle of electromagnetic fields will accelerate protons to almost the speed of light. Then they will crash into a wall of graphite, creating protons and other particles. These particles will decay creating a neutrino stream that will be studied before being fired off through the Earth's crust 800 miles to the Homestake Mine in South Dakota. There they will collide with four tanks the size of warehouses containing super cooled argon. When the neutrinos reach South Dakota and collide with the argon atoms, they should release bursts of light and a large number of electrons. The departing and arriving neutrinos could be compared for differences in quark flavors and how neutrinos move through space and matter. Already knowing about the electron, muon, and tau neutrinos, it would be possible to see if a fourth type existed, the sterile neutrino, so named because, if it exists, it doesn't interact with any matter. Were this neutrino to exist, it is a candidate for dark energy and/or dark matter.[192]

It is interesting theologically that in creating the universe, God made the neutrino, for it is one of the very difficult units to measure and also to capture. Unbelievably fast, charging through almost anything, elusive and

Section Three: Some Recent Scientific Discoveries of Interest and Importance

tricky, the neutrino leads physicists on a merry chase. It is understood but very difficult to study. Maybe that's what its existence was meant to tell us?

CHAPTER 44

Neutrinos and the Urca Process

NEUTRON STARS ARE COLLAPSED remains of supernovas of insufficient size to become black holes. "They are the smallest and densest stars . . . usually have a diameter of 20 kilometers and are so dense that a single teaspoon containing neutron star material would weight nearly 1 billion tons." In a super nova explosion, "the hot remnant—produced after the stellar core collapses—is so dense that most electrons and protons merge to form neutrons." They shed neutrinos in the Urca process, named after a Rio de Janeiro casino George Gamow and Mário Schenberg visited. One remarked that the process that removes heat from supernovas does so as swiftly as those casino tables remove tourists's money.[193]

Edward Brown at Michigan State University has studied a neutron star 35,000 light-years from Earth. As the star cooled, the rate of cooling was found to parallel the *direct* Urca process "between its feeding sessions. Neutrinos carried away energy about 10 times faster than the rate of energy is radiated by the sun's light—or about 100 million times quicker than the slow process." Other neutron stars have seemed to hint at such a cooling down, but "this is basically the first object for which we can see the star actually cooling before our eyes" according to James Lattimer of Stony Brook University of New York. Neutrinos generated inside a neutron star react with matter very rarely, rapidly escaping, cooling the neutron star.[194]

Neutron stars spin exceedingly rapidly, primarily because of their small size but gigantic mass (about 900 times the Great Pyramid of Egypt) and weight about fifteen times the weight of the Moon. "Thus, by conservation

Section Three: Some Recent Scientific Discoveries of Interest and Importance

of angular momentum, neutron stars spin very fast. Typical rotational periods are of the order of seconds. However, some neutron stars spin much faster. One . . . spins 716 times a second . . ."[195]

Neutron stars cool down in several ways; one is by conduction, where heat is transferred by direct contact; second is by convection, where heat is transferred from a "hot part of a fluid to a cooler part through actual movement of mass"; third is radiation, "where heat is given off by a hot body in waves of electromagnetic radiation."[196] This third type of cool down is that previously mentioned above, the direct Urca process where the particles are primarily neutrinos.

This direct Urca process is the simplest and fastest method by which neutron stars can cool down. A neutron star with an initial temperature of 100 billion to even one trillion Kelvin can, by utilizing the direct Urca, cool down to one billion Kelvin in the order of minutes. Later, the modified, slower Urca process takes over. One neutron star has been studied sufficiently to propose that it went through the direct Urca process. This star is MXB 1659–29, a binary pair with one being a neutron star. Studies of the emissions revealed "that MXB 1659–29 has indeed, during its formative years, gone through a phase of enhanced cooling via the direct Urca process."[197]

Neutrinos and the Urca Process

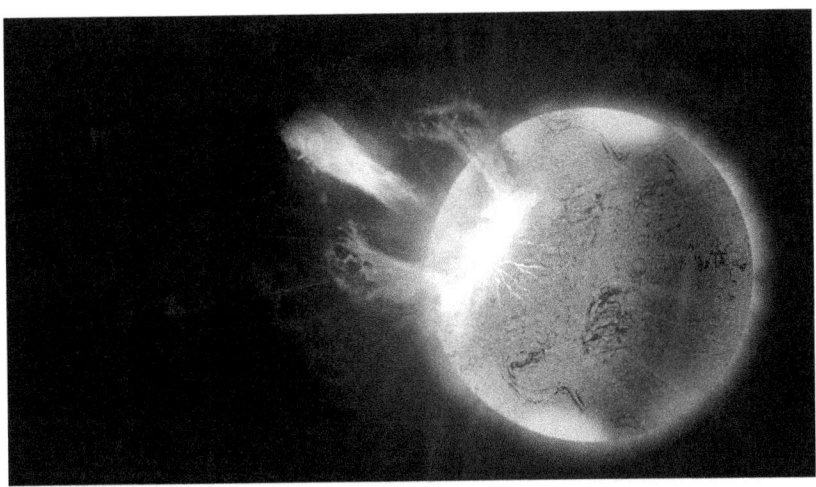

A rupture in the crust of a magnetized neutron star, in an artist's rendering, can trigger eruptions. (NASA's Goddard Space Center/S.Wiessinger) A Magnetar SGR 1806-20 had a burst where in one-tenth of a second it released more energy than the Sun has emitted in the last 100,000 years.

This image shows a neutron star shedding neutrinos similar to the Urca process. Matter is quickly converted to energy—neutrinos.

A new Urca process has also been discovered in the process of core silicon-burning massive stars.[198] Beside the fast and slow, there may be more Urca processes still not discovered.

The Urca process which cools down the heat of neutron stars is interesting, for its direct process, which is very fast, seems to be followed by a slower, modified application. Even so, the Urca process does represent how some stars die. The transformation of mass to energy is analogous to the transformation in human death; first, direct and rapid, then it is modified and slower after the initial direct process, with human mass becoming energy.

Having gained a fundamental idea of particles of energy such as neutrinos and how these are shed through the Urca process, there seems to be another piece of our puzzle in the following chapters to grasp and see if it might fit one of our major theological conundrums—what happens materially when we die.

CHAPTER 45

Survival of Information

WITH BLACK HOLES SWALLOWING star systems and neutron stars doing so to their companion stars, you have to wonder what happens to information in the universe when it is devoured. When black holes were first discovered, it was thought that nothing came out of them if light itself could not. This would mean that any information going into the black hole would be lost.

Stephen Hawking, in his final years, was most interested in black holes and how information fared when the holes absorbed it. In studying this question, he wrote in his final book, *Brief Answers to the Big Questions*:

> ... [O]ne can't tell from the outside what is inside a black hole, apart from its mass, electric charge and rotation. This means that a black hole must contain information that is hidden from the outside world. But there is a limit to the amount of information one can pack into a region of space. Information requires energy, and energy has mass by Einstein's famous equation, $E = mc^2$. So, if there were too many bits of information in a region of space, it will collapse into a black hole, and the size of the black hole will reflect the amount of information.[199]

Later in 1974, Hawking found that a black hole seemed to emit particles "at a steady rate" and that the "outgoing particles have a spectrum that is precisely thermal."[200] Hawking argues that "one way to understand the emission from black holes" is the following:

> Quantum mechanics implies that the whole of space is filled with pairs of virtual particles and antiparticles that are constantly

Survival of Information

materializing in pairs, separating and then coming together again, and annihilating each other. These particles are called virtual, because, unlike real particles, they cannot be observed directly with a particle detector. Their indirect effects can nonetheless be measured, and their existence has been confirmed by a small shift, called the Lamb shift, which they produce in the spectrum energy of light from excited hydrogen atoms. Now, in the presence of a black hole, one member of the pair of virtual particles may fall into the hole, leaving the other member without a partner with which to engage in mutual annihilation. The forsaken particle or antiparticle may fall into the black hole after its partner, but it may also escape to infinity, where it appears to be radiation emitted by the black hole.[201]

"As particles escape from a black hole, the hole will lose mass and shrink. This will increase the rate of emission of particles."[202]

After theorizing about these particles falling into black holes, Hawking at first concluded that particles that come out of a black hole seem to be completely random and to bear no relation to what fell in. It appears that the information about what fell in is lost. Hawking explained his concern:

> [F]or years no one suggested a mechanism by which it [information] could be preserved. This apparent loss of information, known as the information paradox, has troubled scientists for the last forty years, and still remains one of the biggest unsolved problems in theoretical physics.[203]

The particles radiating from the black hole (Hawking radiation) seemed "featureless and dull," thermal radiation, which is heat; however, when matter falls into a black hole, it "carries information, in its very structure, its organization, its quantum state—in terms of statistical mechanics, its accessible microstates." The missing information beyond the black hole's event horizon might be still there though inaccessible, so it wasn't destroyed, just beyond reach and not to be worried about.[204]

The radiation from the black hole seemed to carry no information, but if the black hole dissolved, as Hawking theorized, where was the information? Hawking felt it most important to find out whether information did survive in black holes or not. The reason for doing so was most crucial:

> According to quantum mechanics, information may never be destroyed. The deterministic laws of physics require the states of a physical system at one instant to determine the states at the next instant; in microscopic detail, the laws are reversible, and

> information can be preserved . . . Hawking was the first to state firmly—even alarmingly—that this was a problem challenging the very foundations of quantum mechanics. The loss of information would violate unitarity, 'the principle that probabilities must add up to one. 'God not only plays dice, He sometimes throws the dice where they cannot be seen.'[205]

Recent findings and theories about "the unification of gravity and quantum mechanics" have led to "the understanding of the symmetries of space-time." Symmetry has several types: translational and rotational, which are the types "found in 'flat' space-time, the space–time one finds in the absence of any matter." "If one puts objects into space–time, the translational and rotational symmetries get broken. Introducing objects into a space-time is what produces gravity." "Flat" space-time is absent of matter, but most of the universe is filled with matter, perhaps dark matter, thus transitional and rotational symmetry is broken.[206]

Black holes pose a problem for symmetries, but at a black hole, the gravity is most intense and "space-time is violently distorted." Symmetries are broken; however, when you move away from the black hole, "the curvature of space-time gets less and less, [from the decrease of gravity] and very far away," then, "space-time looks very much like flat space-time." Hermann Bondi, A. W. Kenneth Metzner, M. G. J. van der Burg and Rainer Sachs discovered that "space-time far away from any matter has an infinite collection of symmetries known as supertranslations." Each supertranslation has a "conserved quantity . . . that does not change as the system evolves." . . . "What was remarkable about the discovery of supertranslations is that there are an infinite number of conserved quantities far from a black hole."[207]

Hawking used these ideas, along with Malcolm Perry and Andy Strominger, "to find a possible resolution to the information paradox." They knew black holes had "three discernable properties:" mass, charge and angular momentum. They found that black holes had supertranslational charges," which also might allow the preservation of some information. Hawking noted:

> It is likely that these supertranslational charges do not contain all of the information, but the rest might be accounted for by some additional conserved quantities, superrotation charges, associated with some additional related symmetries called superrotations, which are, as yet, not well understood. . . . If this is right, . . . then perhaps there is no loss of information. These ideas have just received confirmation with our most recent calculations.

Survival of Information

Were Hawking's theories correct, then there is no information lost in a black hole. "Quantum mechanics continues to hold, and information is stored on the horizon, the surface of the black hole."[208]

This position of Hawking's on information preservation was his last. The story of how Hawking's mind was changed demonstrates to us how science works, testing ideas and correcting mistakes, then arriving at new insights.

When Hawking published an earlier paper (1975) in *Physical Review*, many "physicists objected vehemently." They realized that in quantum mechanics, information cannot ever be destroyed. One of these was John Preskill at the California Institute of Technology. He argued that "even when a book goes up in flames, in physicists' terms, if you could track every photon and every fragment of ash, you should be able in integrate backward and reconstruct the book." At California Institute of Technology's "Theory Seminar," Preskill warned: "Information loss is highly infectious. It is very hard to modify a little bit of information loss without it leaking into all processes." Preskill made a wager with Hawking that somehow "information must be escaping the black hole." The wager was for an encyclopedia—winner's choice. Leonard Susskind of Stanford agreed: "Some physicists feel the question of what happens in a black hole is academic or even theological, ... not so at all: at stake are the future rules of physics."[209]

In 2004, Hawking reversed his opinions about information loss in black holes, having found a way in which it was possible that quantum gravity is unitary after all and that information is preserved. He applied a formalism of quantum indeterminacy—the "sum over histories" path integrals of Richard Feynman—to the very typology of space-time and declared, in effect, "black holes are never unambiguously black." Hawking had found the answer and wrote: "The information remains firmly in our universe." Hawking conceded the bet and gave Preskill a copy of *Total Baseball: The Ultimate Baseball Encyclopedia*, weighing in at 2,688 pages— "from which information can be recovered with ease," he said. "But maybe I should have just given him the ashes."[210]

Although humorous, this example of scientists carefully working through a problem serves as an example for how science and theology can jointly address major theological questions. If information cannot be destroyed in the universe, if it survives even a black hole, does this discovery not have major importance theologically? What does this principle mean regarding our human deaths?

CHAPTER 46

Perhaps the Greatest Question

IN THE WELL-MADE, INFORMATIVE television series, *The Story of God*, Morgan Freeman asks in the first chapter, "Beyond Death": "The greatest question: What happens when we die?" He reasons this question is a main driving motivation behind religions, perhaps the major one.[211]

Dying is a process and it seems to have two stages: clinical—when the heart stops, and biological—the cessation of brain activity. Up until one dies, the person turns pale from drops in blood pressure, digits become cold or turn blue, pulse becomes slow, and there is marked irregular breathing, becoming slower and slower. When the heart stops pumping oxygen to the brain, the brain cells start to die. Hearing seems to be the last sense to be lost, possibly because "it's the most passive sense." "Even though the whole body may be dead, . . . certain parts within are still alive." The brain is the first organ to break down, and then other organs follow with living bacteria in the body aiding the decomposition process, adding a distinctive odor, which can be smelled even after only a half hour.[212]

At the University of Michigan, a 2013 scientific study found that dying rats had high levels of brain waves just before their hearts stopped. "Researchers believe that the finding could have implications for humans and possibly explain the near-death experiences many cardiac arrest survivors report." The lead author of the report, Jimo Borjigin, PhD, noted: "It [the study] will form the foundation for future human studies investigating mental experiences occurring in the dying brain, including seeing light during cardiac arrest."[213]

Perhaps the Greatest Question

There is little research available that tells us what happens to the mind after death, but a 2014 study may offer some insight. Researchers at the University of Southampton in England examined over 2,000 cardiac arrest patients in the United States, United Kingdom and Austria. Of those who survived, 140 were surveyed about their near-death experiences, and 39 percent reported feeling some kind of awareness while being resuscitated. This sense of awareness included feelings of peacefulness and a sensation that time slowed down or sped up. Thirteen percent reported feeling separated from their bodies, while only two percent experienced full awareness; researchers say this proves that more studies need to be done.[214]

Is this not an area where science and theology can collaborate? Surely it is.

CHAPTER 47

Life After Death—Con

ONE SIDE OF THE argument that consciousness survives after death declares that there is *no* life after death; an afterlife is just impossible. Sean Carroll, a cosmologist and physics professor at California Institute of Technology, argues that human death events happen in the known possibilities. If there were an afterlife, consciousness would have to be something completely separated from human physical bodies, and he believes it is not. He argues that consciousness at a very basic level is a series of atoms and electrons giving us our human mind.[215]

According to Carroll, the laws of the universe would not let our minds operate after our physical demise. "Claims that some form of consciousness persists after our bodies die and decay into their constituent atoms," states Carroll, "face one huge, insuperable obstacle: the laws of physics underlying everyday life are completely understood, and there's no way within those laws to allow for the information stored in our brains to persist after we die." For his evidence, Carroll "points to the Quantum Field Theory (QFT)." In simple terms, the QFT is the belief there is one field for each type of particle. For example, "[A]ll photons . . . are one level, and the electrons, too, have their own field, and for every other type of particle, too. If life continued in some capacity after death, tests on the quantum field would have revealed 'spirit particles' and 'spirit forces.'"[216]

Carroll writes in *Scientific American*:

> If it's really nothing but atoms and the known forces, there would be clearly no way for the soul to survive. . . . Believing in life after death, to put it mildly, requires physics beyond the Standard

Model. Within QFT, there can't be a new collection of 'spirit particles' and 'spirit forces' that interact with our regular atoms, because we would have detected them in existing experiments."[217]

Carroll's argument depends upon not discovering "particles" and "forces" not yet discovered. Interestingly, it was only a year after Carroll stated that argument dependent upon not finding undiscovered particles that the Higgs Boson was finally proven to exist; this long-sought particle adds mass to matter. Carroll, two years later, published his course for The Great Courses on the Higgs Boson.[218] Incidentally, it is very good and informative. Stephen Hawking was also negative on survival after death. In 2011, he stated: "I have lived with the prospect of an early death for the past 49 years. I'm not afraid of death, but I'm in no hurry to die. I have so much I want to do first. I regard the brain as a computer which will stop working when its components fail. There is no heaven or afterlife for broken down computers; that is a fairy story for people afraid of death."[219]

In this interview, Hawking did discuss M-theory, "a broad mathematical framework that encompasses string theory, which is regarded by many physicists as the best hope of yet developing a theory of everything."

Later in the interview, Hawking spoke about the future theorizing:

> One possibility predicted by M-theory is supersymmetry, an idea that says fundamental particles have heavy—and as yet undiscovered—twins, with curious names such as selectrons and squarks. Confirmation of supersymmetry would be a shot in the arm for M-theory and help physicists explain how each force at work in the universe arose from one super-force at the dawn of time.[220]

The introduction of M-theory and supersymmetries increases the possibilities of finding new insights offering possibilities of more information about our universe. M-theory is very new and not yet completely worked out, but it does promise to create interesting possibilities.

CHAPTER 48

Life After Death—Pro

THE QUESTION OF WHETHER or not the theory of quantum mechanics can predict the existence of consciousness surviving after death, although open, is not weighted to the con side; rather, some major minds in theoretical physics argue for the antithetical answer. Prominent physics researchers from institutions such as Cambridge University, Princeton University, and the Max Planck Institute for Physics in Munich claim that quantum mechanics predicts some version of "life after death." They assert that a "person may possess a body-soul duality that is an extension of the wave-particle duality of subatomic particles."[221]

As we have seen, fundamental to quantum mechanics is the concept that there is wave-particle duality—for example, for photons. These particles have the properties of waves but are only realized in the lab as particles. Some physicists now propose that the theory can extend to include soul-body duality as well. The theory claims that quantum mechanics extends to all things, whether living or dead, and if so, then there is life after death "speaking in purely physical terms."[222]

Dr. Hans-Peter Dürr, former head of the Max Planck Institute for Physics in Munich, proposes:

> [A] particle 'writes' all of its information on its wave function; the brain is the tangible 'floppy disk' on which we save our data, and this data is then 'uploaded' into the spiritual quantum field. . . . [W]hen we die, the body, or the physical disk, is gone, but our consciousness or the data on the computer, lives on.

Life After Death—Pro

> What we consider the here and now, this world, it is actually just the material level that is comprehensible. The beyond is an infinite reality that is much bigger, which this world is rooted in. In this way, our lives in this plane of existence are encompassed, surrounded, by the afterworld already ... The body dies but the spiritual quantum field continues. In this way, I am immortal.[223]

It would be helpful to hear from another science—chemistry. Dr. Christian Hellwig, Max Planck Institute for Biophysical Chemistry in Göttingen, has found that the "information in a human central nervous system is phase encoded, a type of coding that allows multiple pieces of data to occupy the same time." Hellwig noted:

> Our thoughts, our will, our consciousness and our feelings show properties that could be referred to as spiritual properties ... No direct interconnection with the known fundamental forces of natural science, such as gravitation, electromagnetic forces, etc. can be detected in the spiritual. On the other hand, however, these spiritual properties correspond exactly to the characteristics that distinguish the extremely puzzling and wondrous phenomena in the quantum world.[224]

Professor Robert Jahn, physicist at Princeton University, concluded: ...

> [I]f consciousness can exchange information in both directions with our physical environment, then it can be attributed with the same 'molecular binding potential' as physical objects, meaning it must also follow the tenets of quantum mechanics. Thus, consciousness can adapt to the tenets of quantum mechanics.[225]

Providing a similar opinion is quantum physicist David Bohm, student and friend of Einstein, who noted: "The results of modern natural sciences only make sense if we assume an inner, uniform, transcendent reality that is based on all external data and facts. The very depth of human consciousness is one of them."[226]

There exists no proof yet of these theories; however, with these claims coming from scientists in physics, one can easily believe them to be consistent with modern scientific theoretical trends and potentially possible to be accepted. Jaime Trosper reported on "how our energy is redistributed after death." Noting that the human body is both energy and matter, Trosper reminds us that our "energy is both electrical (impulses and signals) and chemical (reactions), and that at the present time, you are producing "roughly 20 watts of energy" through our bodies, "enough to power a light bulb." According to the laws of thermodynamics, energy cannot be destroyed; it only changes states. In an isolated system, "the total amount of energy cannot change." Although the universe may be a closed system, "human bodies (and other ecosystems) are not closed—they're open systems. We exchange energy with our surroundings." Trosper noted:

> In death, the collection of atoms of which you are composed (a universe within the universe) are repurposed. Those atoms and that energy, which originated during the Big Bang, will always be around. Therefore, your 'light,' that is, the essence of your energy—not to be confused with your actual consciousness—will continue to echo throughout space until the end of time.[227]

Whether your energy surviving death is not your consciousness is still an open question; however, human beings are, in every sense, bundles of information—from the atoms overlying the quanta to the molecules of elements and electrical charges in nerves included in both body and mind—according to quantum mechanics. Does the universe allow information to disappear or cease to exist? Science says energy continues; it is never lost, and neither is information.

CHAPTER 49

Life After Death—Some Details

FOLLOWING ARE EXCERPTS FROM an interview with Dr. Fred Alan Wolf, physicist at UCLA, a National Book Award winner for his *Taking the Quantum Leap*. He also wrote the highly regarded *The Spiritual Universe: One Physicist's Vision of Spirit, Soul, Matter, and Self*. Wolf has taught at the Universities of London and Paris, the Hahn-Meitner Institute for Nuclear Physics in Berlin, Hebrew University of Jerusalem, and San Diego State University in California. [The interview is abridged.]

> Question: . . . Is there something about "who we are " that is capable of turning into the finer, higher vibrations of the soul?
>
> Dr. Wolf: . . . Plato believed that the physical senses were always going to cloud our perception of the universe. . . . Plato thought that we could never quite experience things as they are 'in reality.' He taught there was a more perfect, non-material realm of experience.
>
> In contrast, Aristotle taught there is no world outside of our senses. . . . [T]he majority of scientists still share Aristotle's basic worldview. I believe that the findings of quantum physics increasingly support Plato. There is evidence that suggests the existence of a non-material, non-physical universe that has a reality even though it may not as yet be clearly perceptible to our senses and scientific instrument. . . . Now most of us were not trained to look for and experience our souls. We've been more or less trained to look for things that can be grasped—things that are physical and solid. But the soul is not tangible, physical or solid. . . . Yet, the soul is an animating principle in the universe more important than anything that is physical or tangible.

Section Three: Some Recent Scientific Discoveries of Interest and Importance

To further explore the possibility of the soul in scientific terms, we can look into the heart of quantum physics. It has been said at the onset that the study of quantum physics is a very difficult realm to investigate because the objects and forces that are studied . . . are usually infinitesimally small. As we go down to the level of sub-atomic particles, scientists find these particles are moving so rapidly that we can't follow them as we would follow an ordinary larger object moving in ordinary space. The movements and properties of these very small objects do not follow the old ways of thinking found in classical physics. . . . So a new form of physics had to be created to adequately account for the phenomena we observed. . . . Quantum physicists have also demonstrated in experiments with sub-atomic particles that certain fields have a kind of intelligence and seem to be able to do things that ordinary fields can't do. . . . Many quantum physicists, including myself, believe that the entire universe, the entire creation, was created out of the 'absolute nothingness of the vacuum of space.' It appears this 'vacuum of nothingness' is intelligent, active, and has a consciousness. The source of the soul proceeds from, and is present in, this vacuum. . . . There is no place inside your body where 'you' actually exist. You don't have a particular volume of space or spot that is 'you.' It is an illusion to think that everything outside the volume of space is 'not you'—what you commonly say is 'outside of you.' The best description we can give for this sense of presence is that . . . 'You are everywhere.' The main reason that you have more awareness of being in a body is simply because the sensory apparatus of the body commands a great deal of your attention and that much of your attention is linked to your physical senses. We have an illusion that our human bodies are solid, but they are over 99.99% empty space.

If an atom is blown up to the size of an entire football stadium, the dense part of the atom would be comparable to the size of a single grain of rice placed on the 50-yard line. Now, why is this important? Because in an atom, the nucleus accounts for 99.99% of all the matter or mass. Atoms are mostly made of space. So although we experience ourselves as being solid human bodies, it's more like 'who we are' is an awareness or consciousness that lives in space. . . . Though all material objects cannot, by definition, travel faster than the speed of light, there is evidence that the soul, which is non-physical and therefore not confined by movements in the material world, *can* travel faster than the speed of light . . . called 'superluminal speed.' So at the time of death, . . . it may well be that the person transitions from the material world . . . to a

Life After Death—Some Details

world that operates faster than light speed, the so-called 'superluminal' spiritual world. In that transfer, a tunneling effect may take place in much the same way that it appears to take place in what astrophysicists call a "black hole."

Dr. Wolf continues:

> ... Let me offer a speculative but scientifically grounded view of God. First, in speaking about any phenomena, including God, scientists prefer to say that something or someone *behaves* in this way or that way, rather than say that something is or someone *does* this or *does* that. So, using this scientific terminology, how does God *behave* in the universe? Well, if we read the Bible, God seems to behave in very paradoxical ways. But there is one way that God behaves that seems to be very relevant to this discussion: *God creates*. God is considered the ultimate Creator of all that is. If that's the case, is it possible to speak about 'a physics of God's behavior' that explains how God creates?
>
> Basically, we're looking at a process in which the ultimate source of everything, 'God,' or whatever name you want to call it, transforms consciousness into matter. Once this happens, matter inherently acts as a kind of reflector or mirror of the intelligence from which it sprung. As matter modifies itself over time in an ongoing evolutionary process, new information and intelligence continues to be reflected in an ever-evolving universe.
>
> So what we call God continues to create, with infinite intelligence, every billionth of a billionth of a second, now and for billions and billions of years to come. What is created with this perfect intelligence reflects and modifies everything at every instant and at every level. This happens from the smallest electron to the largest galaxy, including all forms of life in the universe. . . . I don't see the soul and consciousness as an epiphenomenon, or product, of matter. It's just the other way around: I see matter as an epiphenomenon of soul and consciousness. The material world has evolved from the absolute vacuum of space—the home of the soul.[228]

Wolf's concepts undergird theological concepts and deserve our close attention. Non-physicists have also argued that consciousness does survive death. Lynne McTaggar's *The Field: The Quest for the Secret Force of the Universe* does so by positing an underlying energy field that allows non-physical actions of human energy as well as healing and other benefits.[229] Although such a field remains currently unknown in physics, it does provide an interesting question of whether such a field could exist. McTaggar's concepts seem to echo Wolf's.

There seems to be a growing realization among a growing number of scientists that the survival of information after death is necessary scientifically. This contribution of science to theology should not be overlooked by either theologians or persons wrestling with the advent of death.

Chapter 50

Life From Another Perspective

WE'VE SEEN SURVIVAL ARGUMENTS for consciousness after death from the perspective of pro and con, but there is also another perspective where the question becomes entirely irrelevant.

A radical new theory has emerged that states that all you perceive, every bit of it, doesn't exist except "as a result of an active process occurring in your mind." This theory is labeled *biocentrism* and is proposed by Robert Lanza, "named one of *TIME* Magazine's 100 most influential people in the world." Lanza's theory has a central proposal: "Consciousness is creating an awareness of an 'out there' outside of ourselves, when actually, the world we experience around us is actually created in our consciousness. There is no 'out there.'"[230]

His argument is that what we regard as reality, by definition, would have to exist in time and space; however, this is an idea that is meaningless, because "everything you see and experience right now, even your body, is a whirl of information occurring in your mind." Time and space, according to Lanza, "are not absolute realities, only projections of the human and animal minds." Biocentrism relies on the concept that what we call the universe "arises from life and not the other way around." Biology is placed "above the other sciences to develop a theory of everything which comes to the same conclusions as non-duality."[231]

Lanza is not some crackpot writing fantasy. Robert Lanza has been acknowledged as "one of the greatest minds of our times, . . . a noted scientist and foremost stem cell expert . . . [I]n 2014, [he] appeared on TIME's list of the most influential people in the world, . . . was selected as one of *Prospect*

Section Three: Some Recent Scientific Discoveries of Interest and Importance

Magazine's 'World Thinkers of 2015' and . . . has been voted the third most important scientist alive by *The New York Times*.[232]

According to Lanza:

> When we dream our minds use the same algorithms to relate a spatio-temporal reality that is as real, 3-D and flesh-and-blood as the one we experience when we're awake. . . . Death doesn't exist in these scenarios, since all of them exist simultaneously regardless of what happens in any of them. The 'me' feeling is just energy operating in the brain. But energy never dies: it cannot be destroyed.[233]

In an article in *Psychology Today*, Lanza mentions quantum *entanglement*:

> ". . . And how can pairs of entangled particles be instantaneously connected on opposite sides of the galaxy as if space and time doesn't exist? Again, the answer is simple: because they're 'out there'—space and time are simply tools of our mind.
>
> Death doesn't exist in a timeless, spaceless world. Immortality doesn't mean a perpetual existence in time, but resides outside of time altogether. . . . Life is an adventure that transcends our ordinary linear way of thinking. When we die, we do so not in the random billiard–ball–matrix but in the inescapable–life matrix. Life has a non–linear dimensionality—it's like a perennial flower that returns to bloom in the multiverse.[234]

Lanza goes on to describe other physics concepts in defense of this theory. After citing several experiments in quantum mechanics that demonstrate his thesis, he shows how quantum effects are not only miniscule; they enter the observable range:

> . . . [R]esearchers published a paper in *Nature* showing that quantum behavior extends into the everyday realm. Pairs of vibrating ions were coaxed to entangle so their physical properties remained bound together when separated by large distances ("spooky action at a distance," as Einstein put it). Other experiments with huge molecules called 'Buckyballs' also show that quantum reality extends beyond the microscopic world. And in 2005, $KHCO_3$ crystals exhibited entanglement ridges one-half inch high, quantum behavior nudging into the ordinary world of human–scale objects.[235]

All of these indications from the various levels of quantum mechanics demonstrate that the actuality of the universe *might possibly* be as Lanza proposes, although there is a very great deal of research needed to gain such

Life From Another Perspective

a perspective from the viewpoints of most scientists. Lanza's perspective undercuts the very foundations of modern science.

We have seen three separate proposals regarding the survival of consciousness after death: the *Con*, which states that there is nothing after death—our consciousness does not survive; the *Pro*, which posits that there is some evidence we preserve our identity after we die, and Lanza's theory of *biocentrism*, that the entire universe is inside our minds and that life and death do not exist. Scientists are far from proving any of the three proposals, leaving the field open for theological and scientific research to gain further knowledge. It seems that the *Pro* position is gaining more weight with scientists lately, primarily because of the need in theories to preserve information and energy, but we must wait and see.

CHAPTER 51

A View from Analytical Psychology

ANOTHER APPROACH TO THE question of survival of consciousness after death comes from the field of Analytical Psychology. In an interview, when asked whether death was the end, Carl Gustav Jung, founder of Analytical Psychology, replied:

> Yes, if it is an end. And there we are not quite certain about this end because we know that there are these peculiar faculties of the psyche—that it isn't entirely confined to space and time. You can have dreams or visions of the future. You can see around corners and such things. Only ignorants deny these facts. It's quite evident that they do exist and have always existed. Now these facts show that the psyche—in part, at least—is not dependent on these confinements. And then what?
>
> When the psyche is not under that obligation to live in time and space alone—and obviously, it doesn't—then to that extent, the psyche is not submitted to those laws and that means a practical continuation of life of a sort of psychical existence beyond time and space.[236]

The answer, of course, awaits further scientific and theological research. What is apparent, however, is that the idea of death as a non-finality for human consciousness is current in some areas of science, and there are human experiences and knowledgeable scientists of many disciplines that argue for that possibility.

Science continues to explore and discover new realms we have never seen before, new concepts and theories we have never encountered, and new means and instruments for exploration of our universe from its most tiny to its very fartherest realms. In considering the exhausting expanse of what science has so far discovered, from quanta to the boundaries of the amazing and very complex known universe and to the multiple glories in it all formed by their Creator, we must realize that, in facing death, mankind's greatest gift given by our Creator remains hope. That hope is precious, and we must not surrender it to the forces of skepticism and doubt. Science is edging towards some major answers for theology. Shouldn't theology begin getting prepared to include these in its processing to understand its goals?

An Afterword

THIS LITTLE VOLUME HAS argued that theology and science need to reach a new rapprochement. There is much that theology may learn from science, especially physics and astronomy, but also all sciences as well. Such research would aid in allowing theology to confront those latent problems that have existed for our beliefs for far too long.

Several questions arise for science and theology to answer together. What happens to our minds when we die? Since information and energy cannot be lost in the universe, does this mean that our beliefs and our human consciousness, which are also energy, survive?

In answering these questions, would we gain further understanding of the meaning of the Resurrection as an answer to our questions regarding our own eternal survival? Does the promise of Easter for Christians apply to *each* and *every* human being? If so, and it seems it does, then theologically what does that mean for Christians?

If our consciousness survives death, which seems to be true, what does it mean for how we act prior to our deaths?

These questions permeate much of the foundation for Christian faith, but a few theologians are only beginning to tackle them and seek some answers.

One doing so is Catholic theologian, Hans Küng, who's *Eternal Life? Life After Death as a Medical, Philosophical, and Theological Problem*[237] sets out to answer some questions, utilizing research not only from theologians and philosophers, but also from some scientists. His is an example of theology responding to new ideas and an attempt to reconcile older theological thought into modern discoveries. His work is marked by a care not to go beyond the strict boundaries of Roman Catholic official positions, but his is a good start on what needs to be done. Let us hope many others follow his example.

An Afterword

There are still many possible fields of science, especially quantum energy, for theology to explore. The understanding of such possibilities is only in its nascent stages, and so much remains to be discovered. It was only in 2012 that the Higgs Boson, the particle that posits mass, that is substance, was verified. Would it be possible with further breakthroughs that death might be seen as similar to Urca processes, first the direct and then the modified, or possibly other quantum or newly discovered actions not yet discovered?

According to quantum mechanics, information and energy cannot be destroyed. There are bundles of information included inside energy and mass (which cannot be lost, only converted to either one or the other) walking around every day—human beings. If information must survive, then that information survives in our universe, either as energy or matter or both. *Our present understanding of science demands it; scientifically, we survive death.*

It seems obvious that much of what science has discovered in this past incredible century is applicable to aid us in supplying concepts for theologians to consider, ponder further, and possibly use. Our theology is not aided by standing off and regarding modern science as an enemy or an area where the theologian dare not trod. On the contrary, there is much in all the sciences that can help illumine the concepts that confront theology today. If we are "star stuff," if we are indestructible energy and information bundles, then by the rules of modern science, we survive in some form, somewhere, after death. *Vivo Aeternum!*

"*Nihil non ratione traetari intelleginque voluit*"
Tertullian, *De paenitentia*, Ch.1: 2
"There is nothing God does not wish to be
understood and investigated by reason."

Endnotes

1. Fuller et al., *I Seem to be a Verb*.
2. Tyson, *Death by Black Hole*, 113.
3. de la Bédoyère, "Written in Stars," 45.
4. *Calendarium Romanum*, 1969.
5. McMahon, "Saints Removed," *Templar Knight*, Sept. 11, 2011: 1.
6. "Wilfred," *Wikipedia*; *Encyclopaedia Britannica*, "St. Wilfred."
7. *Britannica*, "St. Ursula"; MacMahon, "Saints Removed."
8. *Britannica*, "St. Simeon Stylites"; *Wikipedia*, "Simeon Stylites."
9. *Britannica*, "Magi."
10. *Saturday Evening Post*, Editorial: "We Said It Here First," Nov.–Dec. 2017.
11. Chadwick, "Origen," *Britannica*. All on Origen from this source.
12. MacMullen, *Voting About God*, "Violent," 56–66.
13. *Britannica*, "Second Council Ephesus."
14. Russell, *Heirs to Forgotten Kingdoms*, "Zoroastrian," 75–111; Núñez, "Faith and Fire," 18–29.
15. Jung, *Answer to Job*.
16. *Britannica*, "Pierre Teilhard de Chardin."
17. Rovelli, *Reality is Not*, 259–63.
18. Scharf and Miller, "Zoomable Universe," diagram, 72–73.
19. Netburn, "Cosmic Messenger," 1; Coe, "Back in Time," 40–47.
20. Scharf and Miller, "Zoomable Universe," 72–73.
21. Baggott, *Quantum Story*, 15–16; Rovelli, 2017, 110.
22. Scharf and Miller, "Zoomable Universe," 72.
23. Scharf and Miller, "Zoomable Universe," 73.
24. Rovelli, *Reality Not What It Seems*, 83–86.
25. Rovelli, *Seven Lessons on Physics*, 8–10; *Reality Not What It Seems*, 83–86.
26. Kaplan and Guarino, "Speaking of Science"; Billings, "Cosmic Messengers," 10–12; Betz, "Astronomers See and Hear," 13; Natarajan, "First Monster Black Holes," 29.
27. Rovelli, *Order of Time*, 9–13.
28. Mackey, Damien, "Great Solar Miracle;"; Bennett, Jeffrey. *When the Sun Danced*.
29. Radford, "Fatima Miracle All Wet," 31–33.
30. Heisenberg in Baggott, 92–94.
31. Hawking and Mlodinow, *Grand Design*, 70–72.
32. Baggott, *Quantum Story*, 93–94.
33. Baggott, *Quantum Story*, 96–97.

Endnotes

34. Baggott, *Quantum Story*, 95–105.
35. Baggott, *Quantum Story*, 107–8.
36. Baggott, *Quantum Story*, 110.
37. Baggott, *Quantum Story*, 110.
38. Baggott, *Quantum Story*, 110–1.
39. Baggott, *Quantum Story*, 110–11.
40. Baggott, *Quantum Story*, 115–16.
41. Baggott, *Quantum* Story, 116.
42. Baggott, *Quantum Story*, 119–25.
43. Baggott, *Quantum Story*, 125.
44. Baggott, *Quantum Story*, 41.
45. Betz, "Astronomers See Hear Cosmos," 13.
46. Lorimer and McLaughlin, "Flashes in the Night," 47.
47. Tyson, *Death by Black Hole*, 115–16.
48. Powell, "Constant Fight, 88, 90, 92.
49. Hawking, *Brief Answers*, 4.
50. *Wikipedia*, "List of Buddha Claimants."
51. Werther, "Incarnation"; Thondop, *History Mysticism Tulku Tradition*.
52. Madelung, "Al-Mahdi," 5:1231–38.
53. Friedmann, *Prophesy Continuous*, 121.
54. Martin, "Mahdi."
55. Smith, *Encyclopedia of Baha'i Faith*, 55–59; 229–30.
56. Lohnes, "Siege of Khartoum," *Britannica*.
57. *Britannica*, "Shirk." https://www.britannica.com/topic/shirk.
58. Martin, "Madhi"; Butler, *First Jihad*; Binnuri, "The Maududi Calamity."
59. Martin, "Madhi"; Furnish, *Holiest Wars*; Butler, "The First Jihad"; *Wikipedia*, "Abul A'la Maududi".
60. "Avatar," *Merriam-Webster Dictionary*.
61. Doniger, "Hinduism," *Britannica*.
62. Doniger, "Hinduism," *Britannica*.
63. Doniger, "Hinduism," *Britannica*.
64. Doniger, "Hinduism," *Britannica*.
65. Doniger, "Hinduism," *Britannica*.
66. Jung, *Collected Works*, 18 par. 352.
67. Jung, *Collected Works*, 9ii par. 30.
68. Dundas, "Jainism," *Britannica*; Long, *Jainism: An Introduction*.
69. Dundas, "Jainism," *Britannica*; "Jainism," *Wikipedia*.
70. Dundas, "Jainism," *Britannica*; "Jainism," *Wikipedia*.
71. Dundas, "Jainism," *Britannica*; "Jainism," *Wikipedia*.
72. Dundas, "Jainism," *Britannica*; "Jainism," *Wikipedia*.
73. Dundas, "Jainism," *Britannica*.
74. Dundas, "Jainism," *Britannica*; "Jainism," *Wikipedia*.
75. Dundas, "Jainism," *Britannica*; "Jainism," *Wikipedia*.
76. Hirai, "Shinto," *Britannica*.
77. Hirai, "Shinto," *Britannica*.
78. Hirai, "Shinto," *Britannica*.
79. Hirai, "Shinto," *Britannica*.
80. "Divinity of the Emperor," BBC.

Endnotes

81. Hirai, "Shinto," *Britannica*
82. Weiming, "Confucianism," *Britannica*.
83. Weiming, "Confucianism," *Britannica*.
84. Weiming, "Confucianism," *Britannica*; de Bary, *Sources of Chinese Tradition*; Bloom, "Confucius and Analects," I:41–63.
85. Weiming, "Confucianism," *Britannica*; "What are Core Beliefs"; de Bary, *Sources of Chinese Tradition*, 3; Bloom, "Confucius and Analects," I:41–63.
86. "What are Core Beliefs."
87. One of my PhD students, son of a high Communist leader, reported this belief.
88. "Taoism," BBC; Ames, "Daoism," *Britannica*; Stefon, "Dao," *Britannica*.
89. "Mount Tai," *Wikipedia*
90. "Mount Tai," *Wikipedia*.
91. "Mount Tai," *Wikipedia*.
92. "Mount Tai," *Wikipedia*; Ames, "Daoism," *Britannica*.
93. "Taoism," *Ancient History Encyclopedia* "Taoism" 200; Ames, "Daoism," *Britannica*; Stefon, "Dao," *Britannica*.
94. Reninger, "Eight Immortals."
95. "Sikhism," BBC; "Sikhism," *Wikipedia*; McLeod, "Sikhism."
96. "Sikhism, " BBC; McLeod, "Sikhism," *Britannica*.
97. "Sikhism," BBC; "Sikhism," *Wikipedia*
98. "Sikhism," BBC; "Sikhism," *Wikipedia*.
99. "Sikhism," BBC; "Sikhism," *Wikipedia*.
100. "Sikhism," BBC; McLeod, "Sikhism," *Britannica*.
101. "Sikhism," BBC; McLeod, "Sikhism," *Britannica*.
102. "Sikhism," BBC; "Sikhism," *Wikipedia*.
103. "Sikhism," BBC; "Sikhism," *Wikipedia*.
104. "Sikhism," BBC; "Sikhism," *Wikipedia*.
105. "Sikhism," BBC: McLeod, "Sikhism," *Britannica*.
106. "Baha'i," Religion Facts; "Baha'i Faith," *Britannica*.
107. "Baha'i," Religion Facts; "Baha'i Faith," *Britannica*.
108. "Baha'i Faith," *Britannica*.
109. "Baha'i," Religion Facts.
110. "Baha'i," Religion Facts.
111. Answers.com, "Core Beliefs Judaism."
112. Answers.com, "Core Beliefs Judaism."
113. Answers.com, "Core Beliefs Judaism."
114. Answers.com, "Core Beliefs Judaism."
115. "List of Messiah Claimants," *Wikipedia*; See also references to "Messiahs" in Lenowitz, *Jewish Messiah*; Berger, *Rebbi, Messiah*; de Lange, *Illustrated History Jewish People*; Castelló and Kapón, *Jews and Europe*.
116. Singer, *Satan in Goray*.
117. "Jesus' Real Name," Thought.com; "Joshua," *Wikipedia*.
118. Pelikan and Sanders, "Jesus,"; *Britannica*; Russell, *Heirs to Forgotten Kingdoms*, "Samaritans," 148–89.
119. Perowne, "Herod."
120. "Jesus' Real Name," Thought.com.
121. Torjeson, "When Women Priests" and "Sanctuary"; Eisen, "Women Office Holders"; Clark, *Women in Early Church*.

Endnotes

122. Pius IX, "Eneffabilis Deus."
123. Blakemore, "Ireland Turned Fallen Women."
124. Berenbaum, "Anti-Semitism," *Britannica*; Reich, "Seventy-five years."
125. de Lange, *Illustrated History Jewish People*, 40–43.
126. *Wikipedia*, "List of Messiah Claimants."
127. *Christian History* magazine-Sifting-Christ-controversies-Docetists.
128. *Christian History* magazine-Sifting-Christ-controversies-Apollinarians.
129. *Christian History* magazine-Sifting-Christ-controversies-Modalists
130. *Christian History* magazine-Sifting-Christ-controversies-Ebionites.
131. *Christian History* magazine-Sifting-Christ-controversies-Adoptionists.
132. *Christian History* magazine-Sifting-Christ-controversies-Arians.
133. *Christian History* magazine-Sifting-Christ-controversies-Monophysites or Eutychians.
134. *Christian History* magazine-Sifting-Christ-controversies-Nestorians.
135. "Blessed Trinity," *Catholic Encyclopedia*.
136. "Council of Chalcedon," Gotquestions.
137. "Pierre Teilhard de Chardin," *Britannica*.
138. Paul, "Is Rohr's Christ Christian?"
139. Paul, "Is Rohr's Christ Christian?"
140. Montenegro, "What Do Men Say?"
141. Hawking, *Brief Answers*, 25.
142. Baggott, *Quantum Story*, 15–16.
143. Scharf and Miller, "Observable Universe," diagram, 72–73.
144. Baggott, *Quantum Story*, 20.
145. Baggott, *Quantum Story*, 38
146. Baggott, *Quantum Story*, 122, figure 5.
147. Baggott, *Quantum Story*, 122, figure 5; Hanson and Shalm, "Spooky Action," 58–65.
148. Baggott, *Quantum Story*, 324–25, see note 10; Hansom and Shalm, "Spooky Action," 58–65.
149. Hawking, *Brief Answers, Big Questions*, 52.
150. Baggott, *Quantum Story*, 325, see note 10 and 363, note 4.
151. JPL Newsroom, "Cosmic Magnifying Glasses."
152. Overby, "Have Dark Forces Messing," *New York Times*. D 1.
153. Overby, "Have Dark Forces Messing," *New York Times*. D 1.
154. Overby, "Have Dark Forces Messing," *New York Times* D 1. Jones, "Basics of String Theory," Thoughtco; also Jones, *Basics of String Theory for Dummies*.
155. Overby, "Have Dark Forces Messing," *New York Times*. D 1; Jones, "Basics of String Theory" and "Basics of String Theory for Dummies," Thoughtco.
156. Overby, "Have Dark Forces Messing," *New York Times*. D 1.
157. Cendes, "WTF Are FRBs?" 34–39; Moskowitz, "Inner Lives Neutron Stars," 26.
158. Cendes, "WTF Are FRBs?" 36.
159. Cendes, "WTF Are FRBs?" 36–39.
160. Cendes, "WTF Are FRBs?" 37–39; Katie Peek, "Fast Radio Bursts Grow Up," *Scientific American*, 20.
161. Cerdea, "WTF Are FRBs?" 37; Katie Peek, "Fast Radio Bursts Grow Up," *Scientific American*, 20.
162. Andrews, "Space: Sourcing a Mystery," 48; Katie Peek, "Fast Radio Bursts Grow Up," *Scientific American*, 20.

Endnotes

163. Goodreads.com/quotes, Carl Sagan.
164. Krauss, *Universe from Nothing*. Goodreads.
165. *Britannica*, "Quark"; Hawking, *Brief History of Time*, 85.
166. Hawking, *Brief History of Time*, 91.
167. Hawking, *Brief History of Time*, 92–93.
168. Hawking, *Brief History of Time*, 93–94.
169. Hawking, *Brief History of Time*, 95–97.
170. Hawking, *Brief History of Time*, 97–98.
171. Bennett and Turner, "Cosmic Questions," foldout diagram; immediately following highlighted questions and answers are from this diagram.
172. Bennett and Turner, "Cosmic Questions," foldout diagram.
173. Bennett and Turner, "Cosmic Questions," foldout diagram.
174. Bennett and Turner, "Cosmic Questions," foldout diagram.
175. Betz, "Astronomers See and Hear Cosmos," 13; Natarajan, "First Monster Black Holes," 29.
176. Nadis, "Ripple Effect," 50–52; "Black Holes," 52.
177. Nadis, "Ripple Effect," 52.
178. Nadis, "Ripple Effect," 53.
179. Nadis, "Ripple Effect," 53.
180. Nadis, "Ripple Effect," 54.
181. Nadis, "Ripple Effect," 54.
182. Nadis, "Ripple Effect," 56.
183. Nadis, "Ripple Effect," 56.
184. Nadis, "Ripple Effect," 57.
185. Nadis, "Ripple Effect," 57.
186. Devlin, "Black Hole Picture Captured," *The Guardian*.
187. Devlin, "Black Hole Picture Captured," *The Guardian*.
188. Andrews, "Learning to Speak Neutrino," 48–49; "Sourcing a Mystery," 52.
189. Tyson, *Astrophysics for People*, 91–92.
190. Kumar, "How Neutrinos Formed Detected."
191. Andrews, "Learning to Speak Neutrino, 49.
192. *Wikipedia*, "Deep Underground Neutrino Experiment"; Lackey, "Secrets of Universe," *USA Today*.
193. Nerdruid, "Direct Urca Neutron Stars."
194. Nerdruid, "Direct Urca Neutron Stars."
195. Nerdruid, "Direct Urca Neutron Stars."
196. Nerdruid, "Direct Urca Neutron Stars."
197. Nerdruid, "Direct Urca Neutron Stars."
198. Aulderheide et al. "A New Urca Process," 257–62.
199. Hawking, *Brief Answers Big Questions*, 112.
200. Hawking, *Brief Answers Big Questions*, 113.
201. Hawking, *Brief Answers Big Questions*, 115.
202. Hawking, *Brief Answers Big Questions*, 117.
203. Hawking, *Brief Answers Big Questions*, 119.
204. Gleick, *Information*, 35–8.
205. Gleick, *Information*, 358.
206. Hawking, *Brief Answers Big Questions*, 119–20.

Endnotes

207. Hawking, *Brief Answers Big Questions*, 120–1.
208. Hawking, *Brief Answers Big Questions*, 121–22; for other theories on overcoming the information paradox, see: Giddings, "Escape from Black Hole," *Scientific American*, 51–57.
209. Gleick, *Information*, 358.
210. Gleick, *Information*, 359.
211. *Story of God*, video, Season 1, Chapter 1.
212. Welch, "Things Doctor Won't Tell."
213. Welch, "Things Doctor Won't Tell."
214. Welch" Things Doctor Won't Tell."
215. Carroll, "Physics Immortality of Soul," 11.
216. Carroll, "Physics Immortality of Soul," 11.
217. Carroll, "Physics Immortality of Soul," 11; "There is NO life after death."
218. Carroll, *The Higgs Boson and Beyond*, Great Courses 2015.
219. Hawking, "There is No Heaven."
220. Hawking, "There is No Heaven."
221. Tracy, "Physicist Claim Consciousness Quantum."
222. Tracy, "Physicist Claim Consciousness Quantum."
223. Tracy, "Physicist Claim Consciousness Quantum."
224. Tracy, "Physicist Claim Consciousness Quantum."
225. Tracy, "Physicist Claim Consciousness Quantum."
226. Tracy, "Physicist Claim Consciousness Quantum."
227. Trosper, "The-science-of-death" (2013).
228. Fred Alan Wolf, "Soul and Quantum Physics," 245–52.
229. McTaggert, *The Field*, 3–73.
230. Brown, "Biocentrism: No Time, Death."
231. Brown, "Biocentrism: No Time, Death."
232. Lanza, "Is Death an Illusion?"
233. Lanza, "Is Death an Illusion?" See also Lanza, "Myth of Death."
234. Lanza, "Is Death an Illusion?" See also Lanza, "Myth of Death."
235. Lanza, "Is Death an Illusion?" See also Lanza, "Myth of Death."
236. Jung, "Psyche Lives After Death."
237. Küng, *Eternal Life?*

Bibliography

"Avatar," *Merriam-Webster Dictionary*, 2004.
Ames, Robert T. et al. "Daoism," *Encyclopaedia Britannica*. Apr. 28, 2020. https://www.britannica.com/topic/Daoism.
Andrews, Bill, "Space: Learning to Speak Neutrino," *Discover* 40:1, 2019.
———. "Space: Sourcing a Mystery." *Discover* 40:1, 2019.
Aulderheide, Maurice et al, "A New Urca Process," *Astrological Journal*. 424:1 DOI:10:1086/172887.
Baggott, Jim. *Quantum Story: History in 40 Minutes*. Oxford University Press, 2011.
"Baha'i," modified Nov. 30, 2016. https://www.religionfacts.com/Baha'i.
"Baha'i Faith," Oct. 19, 2020. *Encyclopaedia Britannica*. https://www.britannica.com/topic/Baha'i-Faith.
Basham, Arthur Llewellyn, "Hinduism," Aug. 4, 2019. *Encyclopaedia Britannica*. https://www.britannica.com/topic/Hinduism.
Bauer, Walter. *Orthodoxy and Heresy in Earliest Christianity*. Edited by Robert Kraft and Gerhard Krodel. Philadelphia: Fortress, 1971.
Bennett, Charles and Michael Turner, "Cosmic Questions, *National Geographic* 225:4. Apr. 2014, foldout in Bhattacharjee, *National Geographic*.
Bennett, Jeffrey S. *When the Sun Danced: Myth, Miracles and Modernity in Early Twentieth-Century Portugal*. Charlottesville: University of Virginia Press, 2012.
Berenbaum, Michael, "Anti-Semitism." Modified April 21, 2020. http://www.britannica.com/topic/anti-Semitism.
Berger, David. *The Rabbi, the Messiah and the Scandal of Orthodox Indifference*. Littman Library of Jewish Civilization. Liverpool University Press, 1998.
Berner, Leila Gal. "Yigdal,"https://www.reconjstructioningjudaism.org/document/yigdal.
Betz, Eric. "3 Astronomers See and Hear Cosmos," *Discover* 39:1, Jan.-Feb. 2018, 13.
Bhattacharjee, Yudhijit, "Cosmic Dawn," *National Geographic* 225:4, Apr. 2014, 76–85.
Billings, Lee, "Cosmic Messengers," *Scientific American* 318:1, Jan. 2018.
Binnuri, Allaamah Mohammad Yusuf, "The Mudadudi Calamity," translated editorial in *The Bayyinaat*, June 1, 2018. http://www.Islam Reigns/Jamaate- E-Islam/Mudadudi.
Blakemore, Erin, "How Ireland Turned 'Fallen Women' Into Slaves," *History*, Mar. 12, 2018, updated July 24, 2019. https://www.history.com/news/Magdalene-laundry-Ireland-asylum-abuse.
"Blessed Trinity," Catholic/org/encyclopedia/view.php?id=5222.
Bloom, Irene, "Confucius and the Analects." In *Sources of Chinese Tradition*, edited by William Theodore de Bary, 41–63. New York: Columbia University Press, 1960.

Bibliography

Brown, Justin, "Biocentrism: There's No Time and No Death," updated June 25, 2019. https://ideapod.com/new-theory-based-quantum-physics-says-there's-no-time-no-death.

Butler, Daniel Allen. *The First Jihad: The Battle for Khartoum and the Dawn of Militant Islam*. Philadelphia: Casemate, 2018.

Calendarium Romanum. Liberia Editorice Vaticana: Catholic Church, 1960.

Cameron, Layne. "New Microscope Captures Movements of Atoms and Molecules," National Science Foundation Nov. 23, 2013, from Michigan State University.

Carroll, Sean. *The Higgs Boson and Beyond*. The Great Courses: Chantilly, VA 2015.

——. "Physics and the Immortality of the Soul," *Scientific American*, "Guest Blog," 313:11, May 23, 2011; "There is NO life after death: Scientist insists afterlife is IMPOSSIBLE." EXPRESS.co.uk/life-after-death-what-happens-when-we-die-quantum-physics.

Castelló. Elena Romero and Uriel Macías Kapón. *The Jews and Europe: 2,000 Years of History*. Edison, NJ: Chartwell, 1994.

"Blessed Trinity," Catholic/org/encyclopedia/view.php?id=5222.

Cendes, Yvette, "WTF Are FRBs?" *Discover* 40:2, Mar. 2019.

Chadwick, Henry, "Origen." *Encyclopaedia Britannica*, modified Apr. 23, 2020. https://www.britannica.com/biography/Origen.

Charbonier, Jean Jacques. *Seven Reasons to Believe in the Afterlife: Doctor Reviews Cases for Consciousness after Death*. Translated by James Cain. Rochester, VT: Inner Tradition, 2015.

Christian History. "Heresy in the Early Church: Church History Infografic-Sifting Through Christ Controversies," 51: *Heresy in the Church*, 1996.

Clark, Elizabeth, ed. *Women in the Early Church: Message of the Fathers of the Early Church*. Wilmington, DE: Michael Glazier, 1983.

Coe, Dan, "Back in Time," *Scientific American*, 319:5, Nov. 2018.

Connolly, Seán, "Hope and Mercy and the 'Miracle of the Sun,'" *Catholic World Report*, Oct. 13, 2017.https://www.catholicworldreport.com/2017/10/13/hope-and-mercy-and-the-miracle-of-the-sun.

Conover, Emily, "*Neutron Stars Shed Neutrinos to Cool Down Quickly,*" *Science News*. 193:9, May 26, 2018.

"Core Beliefs of Judaism," https:/www.answers.com/Q/what-are-the-core-beliefs-of-Judaism.

"Cosmic Questions," *National Geographic*. "Diagram: "How Did Our Universe Begin?" "What is the Shape of the Universe?" "Do We Live in a Multiverse?" How Will It End?" in Yodhijit Bhattacharjee, *National Geographic*, 225:4, Apr. 2014.

"Council of Chalcedon," Jan. 2, 2020. https://www.Gotquestions.org/Council-of-Chalcedon.html.

de Bary, William Theodore, ed. *Sources of Chinese Tradition*. New York: Columbia University Press, 1960.

de la Bédoyère, Guy, "It Was Written in the Stars: 3 "The Gospel Truth?'" BBC History, 2017, 18:9, 45.

de Lange, Nicholas, ed. *Illustrated History of the Jewish People*. New York: Harcourt Brace, 1997.

Devlin, Hanna, "Black Hole Picture Captured for First Time in Space Breakthrough," *The Guardian*. Apr. 10, 2019. https://www.theguardian.com/science/2019/apr/10/black-hole-picture-captured-for-first-time-in-space-breakthrough.

Bibliography

Dimuro, Gina, "Yeshua: Name Jesus' Friends and Family Would Have Called Him While He Was Alive," updated Feb. 21, 2020. https://www.allthatsinteresting.com/Yeshua-Jesus-real-name.

"Divinity of the Emperor," BBC. https://www.bbc.uk/religions/shinto/shintohistory/emperor_1.shtml.

Doniger, Wendy, et al, "Hinduism," *Encyclopaedia Britannica*. modified Aug. 14, 2019. https://www.britannica.com/topic/Hinduism.

Drake, Nadia, "First Ever Picture of a Black Hole Unveiled," *National Geographic*. April 10, 2019. https://nationalgeographic.com/science/2019/04/first-black-hole-revealed-m87-event-horizon-telescope- astrophysics.html.

Dundas, Paul, et. al, "Jainism," *Encyclopaedia Britannica*. modified Sept. 13, 2017. https://www.britannica.com/topic/Jainism.

Eisen, Ute E. *Women Office Holders in Early Christianity*. Wilmington, DE: Michael Glazier, 2000.

Encyclopaedia Britannica, s.v. "Baha'i Faith," modified Oct. 19, 2020. https://www.britannica.com/topic/Baha'i-Faith.

———. s.v. "Magi," modified Dec. 20, 201https://www.britannica.com/topic/Magi

———. s.v. "Pierre Teilhard de Chardin," modified July 5, 2019. https://www.britannica.com/biography/Pierre-Teilhard-de-Chardin.

———. s.v. "Quark," Feb. 15, 2019. https://www.britannica.com/science/quark.

———. s.v. "Saint Simeon Stylites," modified May 6, 2020. https://www.britannica.com/biography/Saint-Simeon-Stylites.

———. s.v. "Saint Ursula," modified Apr. 23, 2020. https://www.britannica.com/biography/Saint-Ursula.

———. s.v. "Saint Wilfred," modified Aug. 13, 2020. https://www.britannica.com/biography/Saint-Wilfred.

———. s.v. "Second Council of Ephesus," modified July 5, 2019. jttps://www.britannica.com/event/Councils-of-Ephesus.

———. s.v. "Shirk," modified Apr. 23, 2020. https://www.britannica.com/topic/shirk.

———. s.v. "Sikhism," modified June 1, 2020. https://www.britammica.com/topic/Sikhism.

Falsani, Cathleen. "In New Book, Richard Rohr Says the 'Universal Christ' Changes Everything," Mar. 3, 2019. https://www.religiousnewsservice.co/2019/03/29.

Freeman, Aaron, "The Physics of Death: The Best Eulogy, According to a Physicist," interviewed by Jolene Creighton, National Public Radio, Oct. 30, 2005.

Friedmann, Yohanan. *Prophesy Continuous: Aspects of Islam and Muslim World*. Oxford University Press, 2003.

Fuller, R. Buckminister, Jerome Agel and Quentin Fiore. *I Seem to be a Verb*. New York: Putnam, 1970.

Furnish, Timothy. *Holiest Wars: Islamic Madhis, Their Jihads and Osama ben Laden*. Westport, CT: Praeger, 2005.

Gates Jr., S. James. *Superstring Theory: DNA of Reality*. Chantilly, VA: Great Courses, 2006.

Giddings, Steven B. "Escape from a Black Hole." *Scientific American* 321:6 December, 2019.

Gleick, James. *Information: History, Theory, Flood*. New York: Vintage, 2012.

Goodreads. www.goodreads.com/quotes-535480-we-are-all-star-dust.

Griswold, Eliza, "Richard Rohr Reorders the Universe, Feb. 2, 2020. https://www.newyorker.com/news/on-religions/Richard-Rohr-reorders-the-universe.

Bibliography

Goodreads. www.goodreads.com/quotes-535480-we-are-all-star-dust.

Hadhazy, Adam, "Dark Matter Horse of Different Color, " in "Off to Glue Factory," *Discover.* 40:9, Dec. 2019.

Hanson, Harold and Krister Shalm, "Spooky Action: Recent Experiments Quash Hope that Unsettling Phenomenon of Quantum Entanglements Can Be Explained Away, *Scientific American* 319:6 Dec. 2018.

Hawking, Stephen. *Brief Answers to Big Questions,* New York: Bantam, 2018.

———. *Illustrated Brief History of Time.* New York: Bantam, 1996.

———. "There is No heaven: It's a Fairy Story," interviewed by Ian Sample. *The Guardian,* May 15, 2011. https://theguardian.com/2011/may15/stephen-hawking-interview-there-is-no-heaven.

Hawking, Stephen and Leonard Mlodinow. *Grand Design.* New York: Bantam, 2012.

Hirai, Naofusa, "Shinto," modified Sept. 2019. https://www.britannica.com topic/Shinto.

Johnson, Paul. *History of the Jews.* New York: Harper and Row, 1988.

Jones, Andrew Zimmerman, "Basics of String Theory," updated Mar. 2, 2019. https://www.thoughtco.com/what-is-string-theory.

———. *Basics of String Theory for Dummies.* Hoboken, NJ: Wiley, 2010.

JPL Newsroom, "Cosmic Magnifying Glasses Find Dark Matter Clumps," Jan. 8, 2020. https://www.jpl.nasa.gov/cosmic-magnifying-glasses-find-dark-matter-clumps.

"Judaism," Answers.com. https://www/Q/what-are-the-core-beliefs-of-Judaism.

Jung, Carl Gustav. *Answer to Job.* Translated by R. F. C. Hull. New York: Meridan, 1960.

———. *Collected Works.* Gerard Adler et al, translated by R. F. C. Hull. Vol. 9, ii. *Aion: Researches into Phenomenology of the Self.* III. "Syzygy: Anima and Animus," Princeton University Press, 1969, 11–22.

———. *Collected Works.* Gerhard Adler et al, translated by R. F. C. Hull. Vol. 18, *Symbolic Life: Miscellaneous Writings.* Princeton University Press, 1969.

———. "Psyche Lives on After Death," Word Press video of interview. Oct. 27, 2010. https://wordpress.com/2010/10/27jung-says-psyche-lives-on-after-death.

Kaplan, Sarah and Ben Guarino. "Speaking of Science: Scientists Detect Gravitational Waves from New Kind of Nova Sparking a New Era in Astronomy, *Washington Post,* Oct. 16, 2017.

Krauss, Lawrence M. "Talk of the Nation," interview with Ira Flatow, Jan 13, 2012. National Public Radio, script.

———. *Universe from Nothing: Why There is Something Rather Than Nothing.* New York: Simon and Schuster, 2012.

Kroeger, Santhosh D. "The Neglected History of Women in the Early Church," *Church History,* 17, 6–11. Reprinted 2017.

Kumar, Santhosh D. "How Neutrinos Are Formed and Detected," Nov. 6, 2020. https://digatash.com/science/physics/how-neutrinos-are-formed-and-detected-quantum-mechanics.

Küng, Hans. *Eternal Life? Life After Death as a Medical, Philosophical and Theological Problem.* Garden City, New York: Doubleday, 1984.

Lackey, Catharine, "Secrets of the Universe May Lie in an Old Gold Mine in South Dakota," *USA Today,* August 9, 2017, updated 6:03 same day.

Lanza, Robert, "Is Death an Illusion? Evidence Suggests Death Isn't the End," Nov. 19, 2011. https://www.psychologicaltoday.com/us/biocentrism/201111/is-death-illusion-evidence-suggests-isn't-the-end.

Bibliography

———. "Myth of Death," Dec. 22, 2013. https://www.psychologytoday.com/us/biocentrism/201312/the-myth-of-death.

Long, Jeffrey D. *Jainism: An Introduction*. London: Tauris, 2009.

Lenowitz, Harris. *The Jewish Messiah: From Galilee to Crown Heights*. Oxford University Press, 1998.

"List of Buddha Claimants," *Wikipedia, The Free Encyclopedia*, https://www.en.wikimpedia.org/w/index.php&title?=List_of_Buddha_claimants&oldid=986658921.

"List of Messiah Claimants," *Wikipedia, The Free Encyclopedia*, https://www.en.wikipedia.org/w/index.php?title-List-of-Messiah-claimants-868296738. London: Tauris, 2009.

Lohnes, Kate, "Siege of Khartoum," Mar. 6, 2020. https://www.britannica.com/event/Siege-of-Khartoum.

Lorimer, Duncan and Maura McLaughlin, "Flashes in the Night," *Scientific American*, 318:4, Apr. 2018.

Lutz, Ota. "How Scientists Captured the First Image of a Black Hole," NASA, JPL, California Institute of Technology, Apr. 19, 2019.

MacMullen, Ramsey. *Voting About God in Early Church Councils*. "Violent Element," New Haven, CT: Yale University Press, 2006, 56–66.

Mackey, Damien, "Great Solar Miracle," https://academia.edu/8754527/the-great-solar-miracle-of-fatima-october-13-1917.

Madelung, Wilfred, ed. "Al-Madhi," *Encyclopedia of Islam*. 2nd. ed. Leiden, Netherlands: Brill Academic, 2007, 5:1231–38.

Mark, Joshua J. "Lao-Tzu," *Ancient History Encyclopedia*, modified July 9, 2020. https://www.ancient.en/Lao-Tzu.

Martin, Richard D. ed. "Madhi," *Encyclopedia of Islam and the Muslim World*. New York: Thompson Gale, 2004.

McLeod, William Hewitt. "Sikhism," *Encyclopaedia Britannica*, modified June 1, 2020. https://www.britannica.com/topic/Sikhism.

McLeod, S. A. "Carl Jung," May 21, 2018. *Simply Psychology*. https://www.simplypsychology.org/carl-jung.html.

McMahon, Tony, "Saints Removed by the Catholic Church," *Templar Knight*, Sept. 18, 2011, 1.

McTaggart, Lynne. *The Field: Quest for the Secret Force of the Universe*. New York: Harper Collins, 2002.

Mendes-Flohr, Paul, "Judaism." *Worldmark Encyclopedia of Religious Practices*, Thomas Riggs, ed. "Central Doctrines." digitized Aug. 9, 2010. Farmington Hills, MI. https://encyclopedia.com/religion/Judaism.

Montenegro, Marcia, "What Do Men Say That I Am?" Apr. 2019. https://www.christiananswersforthenewage.org/articles-universalchrist.aspx?sty=ptn.

Moskowitz, Clara, "The Inner Lives of Neutron Stars," *Scientific American* 320:3, March 2019.

Mududi, Syed. "Tajdeed-o-Ahua-e-Deen," Lahore: Chapteter, found in Richard C. Martin ed. "Madhi," *Encyclopedia of Islam and the Muslim World*. New York: Thompson Gale, 2004.

Nardis, Steve, "Ripple Effect," *Discover* 40:4, May 2019.

Natarajan, Priyamvada, "First Monster Black Holes," *Scientific American* 318:2 Feb. 2018.

Bibliography

Nerdruid. "Direct Urca: How Thieving Neutrinos Cool Neutron Stars," May 21, 2018. https://Nerdruid.com/druidcraft/science/physics/astrophysics/direct-urcas-neutron-stars-cooling.

Netburn, Deborah, "Cosmic Megamerger, " *Los Angeles Times* found in *Minneapolis Star Tribune*, "Science and Health," May 27, 2018, SH 1–1.

Novak, David et al, "Judaism," Jan. 23, 2020. https://www.britannica.com/topic/Judaism.

Núñez, Juan Antonio Alvares-Pedrosa, "Faith and Fire: Teaching of Zarathustra," *National Geographic HISTORY*, 4:4 Sept.–Oct. 2018.

Overby, Dennis, "Have Dark Forces Been Messing with the Cosmos?" *New York Times*, "Cosmic Confusion," D:1 Feb. 25, 2019. https://www.nytimes.com/2019/02/25/science/cosmos-hubble-dark-energy.htm.

OuterPlaces, "We Just Proved There's Life After Death," Nov. 13, 2017. https://www.com/Outerplaces.com/science/item/17068.

Paul, Ian, "Is Richard Rohr's Universal Christ Christian," Apr. 10, 2019. https://www.psephizo.com/review/is-richard-rohrs-universal-christ-christian.

Pelikan, Jaroslav Jan and E. A. Sanders, "Jesus," Sept. 13, 2019. https://www.britannica.com/biography/Jesus.

Peek, Katie. "Fast Radio Burst Grow Up." *Scientific American*, 323:6, Dec. 2020, 16.

Perowne, Stewart Henry, "Herod." Modified Mar. 5, 2020. https://www.britannica.com/biography/Herod-king-of-Judea.

Pius IX, "Ineffabilis Deus, 1854," Updated Feb. 20,2020. Papal Encyclicals Online.

Ponlop, Rimpoche Dzogchen, "Is Buddhism a Religion? No, It's Spiritual but Not Religious," *Lion's Roar* Mar. 2018.

Powell, Corey S. "The Constant Fight," *Discover* Jan.–Feb. 2019, 40:1.

Prebish, Charles S. "Is Buddhism a Religion? Yes: It's About Ultimate Reality," *Lion's Roar* Mar. 2018.

Radford, Benjamin, "Fatima Miracle Claims All Wet." *Skeptical Inquirer*, 43:3 May–June 2019.

Reich, Walter, "Seventy-five Years After Auschwitz," *The Atlantic*, January 2020. https://www.theatlantic.com/ideas/archive/2020/01/seventy-five-years-after-auschwitz-anti-semitism-is-on-the-rise/605452. Reninger, Elizabeth, "Eight Immortals of Taoism," *Learn Religions*. May 12, 2018. https//www.learnreligions.com/the-eight-immortals-of-Taoism-3182605.

Rohr, Richard OFM, "Oneing: Alternate Orthodoxy," 8:1 Spring 2019. theuniversalchrist.cac.org/UCOneing.Rohr5-pdf.

———. *Universal Christ: How a Forgotten Reality Can Change Everything We See, Hope for and Believe*. New York: Congregant, 2019.

Rovelli, Carlo. *Order of Time*. translated by Erica Segre and Simon Carnell. New York: New York: Riverhead, 2018.

———. *Reality is Not What It Seems: Journey to Quantum Gravity*. translated by Simon Carnell and Erica Segre. New York: Riverhead, 2017.

———. *Seven Brief Lessons on Physics*. translated by Simon Carnell and Erica Segre. New York: Riverhead, 2018.

Russell, Gerard. *Heirs to Forgotten Kingdoms: Journeys to Disappearing Religions of the Middle East*. "Samaritans," 148–89, "Zorastrians," 76–111. New York: Basic, 2014.

Sagan, Carl, "Stardust." https://www.goodreads.com/quotes/tag/stardust.

Bibliography

Saturday Evening Post. Editorial: "Is Christmas Too Religious?" Nov. 30, 2017, excerpted from an earlier editorial, "God Rest Ye Merry, Dec. 1967. https://www.saturdayeveningpost.com/2017/11/30.

Scharf, Caleb and Robert Miller, "The Zoomable Universe," *Scientific American*, 317:5 Nov. 2017, 70–75, Diagram: "Observable Universe," 72–73.

Scharping, Nathaniel, "Fermilab's Ghost Hunt, *Discover* 40:3 Apr. 2019.

Seeskin, Kenneth, "Maimonides," *Stanford Encyclopedia of Philosophy*, 2nd. ed. Edward N. Zalta, ed. https://plato.stanford.edu/archives/spr2017/entries/maimonides.

"Sikhism," BBC. modified Nov. 6, 2020. https://www.bbc.co.uk/religion/religions/Sikhism.

Singer, Isaac Beshevis. *Satan in Goray*. Translated by Jacob Stone. New York: Farrar, Straus and Giroux, 1996.

Story of God. Morgan Freeman, narrator. 2016. Season 1, Chapter 1. Series produced by Twentieth Century Fox for *National Geographic*.

Stefon, Matt, "Daoism," *Encyclopaedia Britannica*. 2016.https://www.britannica.com/dao.

Sutherland, Joan. "Is Buddhism a Religion: Yes, No, Kind of: It's a Big Tent," *Lion's Roar* March 2018.

"Tai-Shan," https://www.com/san-shin.org/China-sacred-mtns.html.

"Taoism," BBC. https://www.bbc.co.uk/religion/religions/Taoism/belief/religious-1.shtml.

Thondup, Talku. *Incarnation: History and Mysticism of Tulku Tradition of Tibet.* Boston: Shambhala, 2011.

Torjesen, Karen Jo. *Sanctuary: Women in Leadership in the Early Church.* Scotsdale, AZ: ReWrite, 2000.

———. *When Women Were Priests: Women's Leadership in the Early Church and the Scandal of Their Subordination in Rise of Christianity.* Harper: San Francisco 1995.

Tracy, Janey, "Physicist Claim that Consciousness Lives in Quantum State After Death," June 17, 2014. https://www.outerplaces.com/science/physicists-claim-that-consciousness-lives-in-quantum-state-after-death.

Trosper, Jaime. "The Science of Death (and What Happens to Your Energy When You Die)" Dec. 18, 2013. https://www.futurism.com/rahman-physics-of-dying.

Tyson, Neil de Grasse. *Astrophysics for People in a Hurry.* New York: W. W. Norton, 2017.

———. *Death by Black Hole and Other Cosmic Quandaries.* New York: W. W. Norton, 2007.

Weiming, Tu, "Confucianism," Aug. 12, 2019. https://www.britannica.com/topic/Confucianism.

Welch, Ashley, "10 Things Your Doctor Won't Tell You About Death," *Everyday Health,* updated Apr. 3, 2015. https://everydayhealth.com/news/ things-your-doctor-wont-tell-you-about dying.

Werther, David, "Incarnation," *International Encyclopedia of Philosophy.* Oct.12, 2009. https://www.iep.utm.edu.

"What are core beliefs Confucianism," Sept. 23, 2014, Answers.com/Q/what-are-the-core-beliefs-of-Confucianism.

Wikipedia, Free Encyclopedia. "Abul A'la Mududi." Nov. 25, 2020. https://en.wikipedia.org/w/index.php?title=Abul_A%27la_Maududi&oldid=99061720.

———. "Deep Underground Neutrino Experiment," https://en.wikipedia. org/w/index.php?title=Deep_Underground_Neutrino_Experiment&oldid=992009424.

———. "Jainism," Dec. 2, 2020. hiips://en,wikipedia.org/w/index.php?title=Jainism&oldid=991939625.

Bibliography

———. "Joshua," Nov. 16, 2020. http://www.wikipedia.org/w/index.php?title–Joshua&oldid =3284319.

———. "List of Buddha Claimants." Nov. 2, 2020. https://en.wikipedia.org/w.index. php?title–list–of–Buddhist–claimants&oldid=79779615.

———. "List of Messiah Claimants," Nov. 8, 2020. https://en.wikipedia.org./w/index. php?title–list–of–messiah–claimants&oldid=868296738.

———. "Mount Tai," en.wikipedia.org/w/index.php?title=Mount_Tai&oldid=987403862.

———. "Sikhism," https://en.wikipedia.org/w/index.php?title=Sikhs&oldid=996296445

———. "Simeon Stylites." https://en.wikipedia.org./w/index.php?title–Simeon–Sytlites&oldid =985917797.

———. "Wilfred, "https://en.wikipedia.org/w/index.php?title–Wilfred–oldid=983376689.

———. "Yeshua," Nov. 18, 2020. http://e.wikipedia.org/w/index.php?title–Yeshua&oldid =13395199.

Wolf, Fred Alan, "Soul and Quantum Physics" in Eliot Jay Rosen, ed. *Experiencing the Soul: Before Birth, During Life, After Death* Carlsbad, CA: Hays House, 1998, 245–52.

———. *Spiritual Universe: One Physicist Vision of Spirit, Soul, Matter and Self.* Portsmouth, NH: Moment Point, 1996.

———. *Taking the Quantum Leap: New Physics for Nonscientists.* New York: Harper Collins, 1989.

www.ingramcontent.com/pod-product-compliance
Lightning Source LLC
Chambersburg PA
CBHW051056160426
43193CB00010B/1199